THE DISCOMFORT DIVIDEND

Why the Smartest Thing You Can Do as You Age Is Stop Running from What Hurts

Ken Konet, M.Ed., MBA

Humbolton Press

Copyright

© 2026 Ken Konet. All rights reserved.

Published by Humbolton Press

No part of this publication may be reproduced, distributed, or transmitted in any form or by any means, including photocopying, recording, or other electronic or mechanical methods, without the prior written permission of the publisher, except in the case of brief quotations embodied in critical reviews and certain other noncommercial uses permitted by copyright law. For permission requests, contact the publisher.

ISBN: 978-1-966703-25-9 (Paperback)

Cover design by: Ken Konet & DALL-E

Interior layout by: Isabella Green

First Edition: 2026

Printed in the United States of America

10 9 8 7 6 5 4 3 2 1

Table of Contents

THE DISCOMFORT DIVIDEND 1

Why the Smartest Thing You Can Do as You Age Is Stop
Running from What Hurts 1

Copyright...2

Abstract...8

Introduction 10

How to Read This Book (And Why It's Going to Be
Uncomfortable)...10

Who This Book Is For..10

How This Book Is Structured 11

How to Use the Exercises...12

A Note on Tone..13

PART I: THE CONCENTRATION...14

Chapter 1 15

The Funhouse Mirror..15

The Distillation Process..16

The Science Behind the Shrink...18

The Mirror Moment 20

The Compound Interest of Avoidance 20

Research Spotlight: Personality Stability and the Aging
Trajectory 21

Exercise: The Concentration Audit.......................................22

The Good News (Because There Is Some)............................24

Chapter 2 26

The Intelligence Trap 26

The Smartest Person in the Room Problem 27

What Actually Predicts Wisdom 28

Research Spotlight: The Berlin Wisdom Paradigm 29

The Mirror Moment 31

The Fortress of Logic 31

Exercise: The Evidence Threshold Test 32

The Curiosity Dividend 34

Chapter 3 36

The Stubbornness Muscle 36

The Tenacity Hub 37

Superagers and the Shrinking Brain 38

The Huberman Effect (And What He Didn't Say) 40

Research Spotlight: The aMCC and the Cost of Comfort ...41

The Mirror Moment 42

The Emotional Gym 43

Exercise: The Emotional Gym Log 44

What's Coming Next 46

Chapter 4 48

The Certainty Narcotic 48

Your Brain on "I Knew It" 49

The Fork Inside Your Brain 51

Research Spotlight: The Need for Cognitive Closure 52

The Positivity Trap 53

The Mirror Moment 55

Exercise: The Certainty Inventory 55

The Way Out 58

PART II: THE MECHANICS 60

Chapter 5 61

Distress Tolerance 101 61

What Distress Tolerance Actually Is (And What It Absolutely Isn't)..62

The Escape Response: Faster Than You Think 64

Research Spotlight: The 106-Study Review 65

Why This Matters More After Forty....................................67

The Mirror Moment 68

Exercise: The 10-Second Stay 69

Chapter 6 72

The Ambiguity Frontier..72

The Cognitive Cousin..73

Why "I Don't Know" Feels Like Falling 74

Research Spotlight: The Ambiguity–Wisdom Pipeline......76

The Mirror Moment 77

The Five Flavors of "I Don't Know" 78

Exercise: The Open Question Experiment............................79

Chapter 7 83

The Fork in the Road 83

The Catalyst Theory..84

Grief: The Master Class..86

Research Spotlight: Hard-Earned Wisdom 88

The Ego Question 89

The Mirror Moment 90

Exercise: The Grief Inventory 91

Chapter 8 95

The Social Wall..95

The Fortress That Feels Like a Home..................................96

The Curating Trap..97

The Loneliness Data..98

The Intergenerational Workout 99

The Mirror Moment..100

Exercise: The Conversation Bridge........................100

PART III: THE PRACTICE 103

Chapter 9...104

Sitting in the Fire 104

Arena 1: The Kitchen Table............................105

Arena 2: The News Feed...................................106

Arena 3: The Body's Betrayal..........................107

Arena 4: The Silence Test.................................108

The Mirror Moment...110

Chapter 10...112

The Softened Edge 112

What Happens When You Stop Fighting ...113

The Complexity of Wisdom............................114

Research Spotlight: Cognitive Reappraisal 115

The Mirror Moment...116

Exercise: The Reappraisal Practice 116

Chapter 11...119

Building the Muscle..119

Practice 1: The Pause Protocol.....................120

Practice 2: The "What Would I Need to See?" Exercise...121

Practice 3: The Discomfort Journal..............121

Practice 4: The Perspective Swap 122

Practice 5: The Micro-Suck.............................123

Practice 6: The Novelty Requirement...........123

Exercise: Design Your Practice Plan.............124

PART IV: THE DIVIDEND 126

Chapter 12...127

The Discomfort Dividend..127

Currency One: Better Decisions.............................127

Currency Two: Richer Relationships.....................128

Currency Three: Reduced Death Anxiety.............129

Currency Four: Grace...130

The Mirror Moment..131

Resilience vs. Endurance...132

Chapter 13...134

The Final Unfolding...134

The Garden That Never Stops Growing................135

The Calibration Principle..135

Research Spotlight: The Seeds and the Harvest...137

The Mirror Moment..138

Exercise: The Letter to Your Future Self..............138

What This Book Was Really About...............................141

Appendix A: The Research at a Glance.....................143

Pillar A: The Neuroscience.....................................143

Pillar B: The Psychology...144

Pillar C: Aging and Emotion...................................145

Pillar D: Additional Research.................................146

Appendix B: Recommended Reading.....................147

About the Author...149

Abstract

Aging doesn't change who you are. It concentrates who you are.

The Discomfort Dividend presents a single, research-grounded argument that no other book on aging, wisdom, or personal development has made in trade nonfiction: the primary determinant of whether you age into wisdom or rigidity is your willingness to tolerate emotional discomfort — and this capacity is trainable, measurable, and rooted in specific brain structures.

Drawing on the neuroscience of the anterior midcingulate cortex (aMCC), the FADE neuroimaging hypothesis, the MORE Life Experience Model of wisdom development, a 2025 study linking ambiguity tolerance to wisdom through epistemic curiosity, and a systematic review of 106 studies on distress tolerance interventions, this book translates cutting-edge research into a practical, accessible, and occasionally profane manual for anyone who has noticed themselves becoming a more concentrated version of their worst tendencies — or anyone who wants to prevent it.

Organized across four parts — The Concentration (the problem), The Mechanics (the science), The Practice (the toolkit), and The Dividend (the payoff) — the book offers thirteen chapters of neuroscience, psychology, and instructional-design-driven exercises that teach readers how to stay in the conversations they want to leave, question the beliefs they want to protect, and sit with the discomfort they've spent decades avoiding.

The result is the discomfort dividend: better decisions, richer relationships, reduced fear of death, and the visible quality of grace that comes from a nervous system that has stopped fighting reality and started engaging with it.

This book is for anyone who has ever caught themselves becoming the person who yells at the television — and decided to do something about it before the concrete sets.

Introduction

How to Read This Book (And Why It's Going to Be Uncomfortable)

Welcome. I'm glad you're here. I'm also a little sorry, because this book is going to ask you to do things you don't want to do, feel things you'd rather not feel, and question things you've spent a lifetime believing. And I'm going to do it while cracking jokes, because that's how I process the fact that I have three master's degrees and still can't sit in a quiet room for twenty minutes without reaching for my phone.

My name is Ken Konet. I'm an instructional designer by trade, which means my job is to take complicated things and make them learnable. I've spent my career designing learning experiences for adults — the kind of experiences that don't just transfer information but actually change behavior. That's what this book is built to do. Not inform you. *Change* you. Or at least give you the tools to change yourself, which is the only kind of change that sticks.

Who This Book Is For

This book is for you if:

- You've noticed yourself getting more rigid, more reactive, or more certain with age — and you don't like it.
- You've watched someone you love calcify into a louder, more fragile version of themselves and thought: *How do I make sure that's not me?*
- You're between 40 and 80 and you've started to feel your world getting smaller without choosing for it to get smaller.

- You've ever changed the channel, left the room, or shut down a conversation because it made you uncomfortable — and later wondered what you missed.
- You want the science behind what's happening in your brain as you age, delivered by someone who doesn't talk to you like you're in a lecture hall.
- You're a therapist, coach, or educator who needs a bridge between clinical research and real-world application for the people you serve.

This book is *not* for you if you're looking for a gentle meditation on the beauty of aging. There are lovely books that do that. This isn't one of them. This book has teeth. It has exercises. It has homework. And it has a point of view: comfort is the most dangerous thing you can pursue in the second half of life, and the only antidote is the deliberate, repeated, unglamorous practice of sitting with things that hurt.

How This Book Is Structured

The book is divided into four parts, and they're designed to be read in order. Each part builds on the one before it:

Part I: The Concentration (Chapters 1–4) — *What's happening and why you should care.* These chapters establish the problem: aging concentrates your personality, intelligence can't save you from rigidity, your brain has a trainable muscle for doing hard things, and certainty is the drug that keeps you from growing. By the end of Part I, you'll understand the mechanism of calcification — and you'll probably recognize it in yourself.

Part II: The Mechanics (Chapters 5–8) — *The science and the skills.* These chapters give you the conceptual tools: what distress tolerance actually is (and what it isn't), how ambiguity tolerance predicts wisdom, why the decade between 45 and 55 is the critical pivot point, and how social rigidity leads to isolation. By the end of Part II, you'll have a vocabulary for what needs to change and the research to back it up.

Part III: The Practice (Chapters 9–11) — *Where to do the work.* These chapters are the practical heart of the book. Chapter 9 walks you through the four arenas where discomfort tolerance is built in everyday life. Chapter 10 explains what actually changes in your nervous system when you stop fighting reality. Chapter 11 gives you a six-practice toolkit with specific protocols, frequencies, and instructions. By the end of Part III, you'll have a personal practice plan.

Part IV: The Dividend (Chapters 12–13) — *What you get for staying.* These chapters deliver the payoff: the four domains of the discomfort dividend (better decisions, richer relationships, reduced death anxiety, and grace), the difference between resilience and endurance, and the argument that wisdom is a practice that never ends — and why that's the point.

How to Use the Exercises

Every chapter contains structured exercises designed by an instructional designer (that's me) who believes most self-help exercises are too vague to be useful and too humorless to be tolerable. Each exercise includes:

- **Purpose:** Why you're doing this.
- **Instructions:** Step-by-step. Specific enough to follow. Simple enough to actually do.
- **What You Might Notice:** What typically comes up. This isn't prediction — it's preparation. Knowing what to expect makes it easier to stay.
- **Debrief:** What it means and what to do with it.

The exercises are scaffolded — they start easy (a ten-second pause) and build to hard (a twenty-minute silence with no distractions). You don't have to do every exercise the first time through. But I'd encourage you to try the ones that make you the most uncomfortable. The resistance is the map. The discomfort is the territory. And the dividend is on the other side.

You'll notice this book doesn't sound like most books about aging or wisdom. It's snarky. It's irreverent. It occasionally uses language your grandmother wouldn't approve of. There's a reason for that.

If I'm asking you to sit with discomfort, the least I can do is make the sitting entertaining. Humor lowers defenses. It lets the hard stuff land in places that a lecture can't reach. And honestly, the topic of "you might be turning into a worse version of yourself and your IQ can't save you" is scary enough that somebody in this room needs to be funny about it. I volunteered.

But underneath the jokes, every claim in this book is grounded in peer-reviewed research. Every exercise is informed by evidence-based clinical practice. And every argument is made with genuine care for the person reading it — which is you, and which means I need you to hear this: I'm not making fun of you. I'm making fun of *us*. All of us. The absurd, beautiful, terrifying business of being a human who ages. We're in this together.

Now let's get uncomfortable.

PART I: THE CONCENTRATION

What's happening and why you should care

Chapter 1

The Funhouse Mirror

Aging doesn't change you. It amplifies you.

Let me introduce you to two people. You already know them both.

The first one — let's call him Ed — is seventy-two. He walks into a room and the air gets warmer. Not hotter. *Warmer.* He asks questions. Real ones, not the kind where he's waiting to hear himself talk. He laughs at himself more than he laughs at anyone else. He has friends in their forties and friends in their eighties and he doesn't seem to notice the difference. When his granddaughter explains something about her life that he genuinely doesn't understand — pronouns, cryptocurrency, whatever the hell a "situationship" is — he doesn't get defensive. He leans in. He says, "Tell me more about that." And he means it. When Ed walks out of a room, people feel like they've been *seen*. Not evaluated. Not judged. Seen.

The second person — let's call her Diane — is also seventy-two. Same generation. Roughly similar education, income, neighborhood. Diane walks into a room and you can feel everyone's posture tighten by half an inch. She has opinions. She has *takes*. She has a very specific seat at the table and God help you if you're sitting in it. She hasn't asked a question she didn't already know the answer to since the Bush administration. The first one. When her grandson tries to talk about his life, Diane listens for about forty-five seconds before redirecting the conversation to how things were done in her day, which was better, obviously, because things were always better when the person telling the story was younger. She's not mean. She's not cruel. She's just... *closed*. Like a fist that forgot how to open.

Same generation. Same approximate raw materials. Wildly different outcomes.

And if you're reading this book, there's a very good chance you've been wondering — maybe for years, maybe just recently, maybe in a 3 AM bolt of existential clarity — which one you're turning into.

Here's the part that's going to make you uncomfortable: the answer was decided a long time ago. Not permanently. Not irreversibly. But the trajectory? That's been building since your thirties. And the mechanism behind it is both simpler and scarier than you think.

The Distillation Process

Here's the premise of this entire book in one sentence: **aging doesn't change who you are. It concentrates who you are.**

Stay with me here.

Think about what happens when you boil a pot of broth. The water evaporates. What's left gets thicker, more intense, more *itself*. If the broth was made with good ingredients — rich stock, fresh herbs, patience — what remains is extraordinary. Deep. Complex. Worth savoring. But if the broth was made with shortcuts — bouillon cubes, tap water, and a prayer — what remains when the water evaporates is... well, salty. Thin. Trying very hard to be something it isn't.

Aging is the evaporation process. The water — your energy, your distractions, your busyness, the sheer momentum of a life that hasn't slowed down enough to look at itself — gradually cooks off. And what's left is whatever was dissolved in it the whole time. Every bias you carried at thirty-five. Every avoidance strategy you polished at forty. Every time you

16

changed the channel because the news made you feel something you didn't want to feel. Every hard conversation you walked away from. Every belief you held tighter instead of examining closer. Every moment you chose comfort over curiosity.

It was all dissolving in the broth. And now the water's leaving.

This is why Ed and Diane ended up in such different places despite starting from such similar ones. It wasn't destiny. It wasn't genetics. It wasn't that Ed had a better childhood or a nicer spouse or a sunnier disposition. It was that Ed, somewhere along the line, dissolved different ingredients into his broth. He kept asking questions when it would've been easier to stop. He stayed in conversations that made him squirm. He let himself be changed by new information instead of building walls against it. Not because he's a saint — Ed will tell you himself that he's not — but because something in him resisted the urge to close down when closing down would've been the more comfortable option.

Diane did the opposite. Not dramatically. Not in one big moment. In ten thousand tiny ones. She changed the channel. She left the argument. She curated her friend group until everyone agreed with her. She stopped asking questions she might not like the answers to. She didn't *decide* to become rigid. She just chose comfort, over and over, in small enough doses that she never noticed the compound interest.

And now the water's gone and here they are. Ed is broth. Diane is bouillon.

You know how people say "He really mellowed with age"? That's not mellowing. That's a man who found his couch, his opinion, and his remote, and decided the universe could come to him. That's not evolution. That's a man-shaped recliner. Mellowing is what happens when someone has *processed* enough discomfort that they no longer need to react to it. What most people call mellowing is actually the opposite — it's someone who has avoided enough discomfort that they've lost the capacity to engage with it at all.

The distinction matters. Because the Ed path and the Diane path don't look different from the outside until they're well underway. Both people might describe themselves as "comfortable." Both might say they're "at peace." But Ed's comfort comes from expansion — he's been stretched wide enough by experience that not much rattles him anymore. Diane's comfort comes from contraction — she's narrowed her world until the only things left in it are the things that don't challenge her.

One is peace. The other is a cage that looks like peace from the inside.

The Uncomfortable Truth: You are not aging into someone new. You are aging into a louder version of who you've always been. The behaviors you've been getting away with at low volume for decades are about to get turned up to eleven. The question isn't "who will I become?" It's "what have I been avoiding?"

The Science Behind the Shrink

Let me bring in the researchers for a minute, because this isn't just my opinion. Psychologist Laura Carstensen at Stanford has spent decades studying something called Socioemotional Selectivity Theory — which is a fancy name for a pretty intuitive idea: as people get older and start to sense that their time is limited, they naturally shift their priorities.

Young people optimize for *information*. They want new experiences, new connections, new data. They're building their understanding of the world, so they cast wide nets. They tolerate a lot of discomfort — bad roommates, terrible jobs, awkward social situations — because the potential payoff (learning, growth, opportunity) is worth the investment.

Older people optimize for *emotion*. They've built their understanding of the world (or they think they have), so they start curating for quality over quantity. They spend time with people who make them feel good. They pursue activities they enjoy. They let go of relationships and obligations that drain them without enriching them.

This sounds wonderful. And in many ways, it is. Carstensen's research shows that older adults often report *higher* emotional well-being than younger adults. They experience fewer negative emotions and more positive ones. They regulate their emotional states more effectively. By most measures, they're doing great.

But — and this is a "but" the size of a Buick — there's a catch.

The same mechanism that lets you focus on what matters can also let you *avoid* what's hard. "I'm prioritizing positive experiences" and "I'm refusing to engage with anything uncomfortable" can look identical from the outside. They feel identical from the inside. But the first one is wisdom and the second one is a slow-motion personality collapse.

Carstensen calls the positive version the "positivity effect" — the documented tendency for older adults to preferentially attend to and remember positive information over negative information. It's a real thing. It's measurable. And when it operates through genuine emotional regulation — when a person is *processing* negative information but choosing not to dwell on it — it's one of the legitimate superpowers of aging.

But when it operates through avoidance — when a person is *filtering out* negative information before it can be processed, refusing to engage with anything that might challenge their worldview, surrounding themselves with agreement and calling it contentment — it becomes the mechanism by which the world shrinks. The focusing on the good becomes the refusing to see the bad. And the refusing to see the bad is the first brick in a wall that eventually becomes a prison.

That's the funhouse mirror. Same reflection, two different distortions. And you can't tell which one you're looking at unless you're willing to look very, very closely.

The Mirror Moment

I need you to pause here. Not skim ahead. Not nod thoughtfully and keep reading. Actually pause.

Think about the last time you changed the channel, closed a browser tab, or walked away from a conversation because it was making you uncomfortable. Not physically threatened. Not abused. Not in any danger. Just... *uncomfortable.* The information was challenging. The person was saying something you didn't want to hear. The emotion was one you didn't want to feel.

How often does that happen? Weekly? Daily? Several times a day?

You don't have to answer out loud. You don't have to write it down. Just notice. Hold the number in your head. We'll come back to it.

The Compound Interest of Avoidance

Here's the thing about avoidance that makes it so insidious: it doesn't feel like avoidance. It feels like *preference.*

"I just don't enjoy that kind of conversation." That's avoidance wearing a turtleneck.

"I've earned the right to not deal with things that upset me." That's avoidance in a three-piece suit.

"I know what I believe and I don't need someone half my age telling me I'm wrong." That's avoidance with a mortgage and a voter registration card.

None of these feel like running. They feel like *arriving*. They feel like the natural reward of a life well-lived — the earned right to stop engaging with things that make you uncomfortable. And in a culture that worships comfort the way ours does, who's going to argue? You did your time. You put in the years. You deserve to relax.

Except relaxation and rigidity are not the same thing. Not even close. Relaxation is a state you enter *voluntarily*, knowing you can leave whenever you want. Rigidity is a state you enter so *gradually* that you don't realize you can't leave until someone points out that you've been sitting in the same chair, watching the same channel, talking to the same three people, holding the same twelve opinions, for the last decade.

And the compound interest on this is brutal. Every time you avoid a moment of discomfort, you make the *next* moment of discomfort slightly harder to tolerate. The avoidance muscle gets stronger. The tolerance muscle gets weaker. Your comfort zone doesn't stay the same size — it *contracts*. What was tolerable at fifty becomes intolerable at sixty. What was merely annoying at sixty becomes enraging at seventy. Your world shrinks. Your reactions amplify. Your flexibility decreases.

That's the concentration process. That's the water evaporating. And you are left with whatever was dissolved in the broth.

Research Spotlight: Personality Stability and the Aging Trajectory

Psychologist Brent Roberts and his colleagues published a landmark meta-analysis in *Psychological Bulletin* (2006) examining how personality traits change — or don't — across the lifespan. What they found was both reassuring and alarming. The reassuring part: personality traits are remarkably stable across adulthood. You don't wake up one day as a fundamentally different person. The alarming part: the small changes that *do* occur tend to move in a specific direction. Most people become slightly more agreeable and slightly more conscientious as they age — which sounds great. But they also tend to become slightly less *open*. Less curious. Less interested in novel experiences. Less willing to entertain ideas that don't fit their existing framework.

These shifts are small. In any given year, you wouldn't notice them. But compound them over three decades and you've got a person who has gradually, imperceptibly, narrowed the aperture through which they see the world. Not because they chose to. Because the default direction of aging — without intervention — is toward closure.

The key phrase there is *without intervention*. The decline in openness is a tendency, not a law. Some people buck it entirely. Some people become *more* open as they age. Roberts' data shows enormous individual variation. The question is: what are the people who stay open doing differently?

That's what the rest of this book is about.

Exercise: The Concentration Audit

Purpose: To identify what's "concentrating" in you — the patterns, habits, and avoidance strategies that are quietly amplifying as you age.

Instructions:

1. Get a piece of paper. Any paper. The back of a grocery receipt works. Draw a line down the middle.

2. Left column header: **"Things I did at 30 that I still do at [your current age]."** List behaviors, reactions, opinions, habits, and emotional tendencies. Be merciless

22

here. Include the good ones (I was curious about new music; I could disagree with someone without it ruining my week) and the ones that make you wince (I avoided confrontation; I changed the subject when conversations got too emotional; I assumed people who disagreed with me just hadn't done enough reading).

3. Right column header: **"Louder or Quieter?"** For each item, note whether this behavior has gotten *louder* (more frequent, more intense, more automatic, more defended) or *quieter* (less frequent, more modulated, more intentional, more examined) over the years.

4. Circle every item marked "Louder."

5. Now star every circled item that involves *avoiding discomfort* in some way — changing the subject, leaving the room, refusing to engage, reaching for a screen, doubling down on an opinion without re-examining it, cutting off a relationship instead of having a hard conversation.

What You Might Notice: The starred items are your concentration points. These aren't character flaws. They're not moral failures. They're avoidance strategies that have been earning compound interest for decades. They're the dissolved solids in the broth. The water has been evaporating around them for years, and they're getting more concentrated whether you like it or not.

You might also notice that some of them surprise you. The behaviors you're most worried about (your temper, your impatience) might not be the ones that are concentrating most dangerously. Sometimes it's the quiet ones — the slow withdrawal from new people, the gradual narrowing of your media diet, the almost invisible shift from "I wonder about that" to "I already know about that" — that carry the heaviest compound interest.

Debrief: You don't have to fix anything right now. That's not the assignment. The assignment is to *see*. Awareness is the first deposit in the discomfort dividend account. You cannot change what you refuse to notice, and you cannot notice what you refuse to look at. You just looked. That's the first rep.

The Good News (Because There Is Some)

I've spent this entire chapter telling you that you're slowly turning into a more extreme version of yourself and that the default trajectory of aging is toward closure. I realize this is not a great sales pitch. "Buy this book! You're calcifying!" is not going to win any marketing awards.

So here's the thing I need you to hold onto as we move forward: the concentration process is not destiny. It's *chemistry*. And chemistry can be changed.

The water doesn't have to evaporate around the same old ingredients. You can add new ones. You can change the recipe. You can introduce elements that didn't used to be there — curiosity where there was certainty, flexibility where there was rigidity, presence where there was avoidance. The broth doesn't have to be bouillon. But the window for changing the recipe narrows as the water level drops. Not because it becomes *impossible* — it doesn't; neuroplasticity is real and it persists throughout the lifespan — but because it becomes *harder*. The behaviors that have been concentrating for decades have momentum. Changing them requires effort. And that effort requires a specific, trainable, measurable skill that most people have never been taught and almost nobody talks about.

That skill has a name. It's called distress tolerance. And it is, by a comfortable margin, the most important skill you will ever develop for the second half of your life.

But we'll get to that. First, we need to talk about why your IQ can't save you from any of this.

Chapter Takeaway: Aging doesn't transform you. It distills you. The water evaporates and what remains is whatever you dissolved in the solution your whole life. The default trajectory — without deliberate intervention — is toward concentration, closure, and rigidity. But the recipe can be changed. Awareness is the first ingredient.

The funhouse mirror doesn't distort you. It just shows you the parts you've been pretending aren't getting bigger.

Chapter 2

The Intelligence Trap

Why your IQ can't save you from becoming insufferable.

I once sat across a dinner table from a man with a PhD in economics, a wall of published papers, a jaw-dropping vocabulary, and absolutely zero capacity to consider the possibility that he might be wrong about anything.

We were talking about education policy. I don't even remember the specific issue — something about standardized testing, maybe, or charter schools. It doesn't matter. What matters is what happened when someone at the table offered a perspective that contradicted his. He didn't pause. He didn't ask a question. He didn't even blink. He launched into a twelve-minute monologue that cited four studies, two historical precedents, and a personal anecdote from a conference in Geneva, and by the time he was finished, everyone at the table had the same expression: the glazed, slightly defeated look of people who've realized that this isn't a conversation. It's a lecture with an audience that can't leave because there's still risotto on the table.

This man was, by any measurable standard, brilliant. His IQ was probably in the 140s. He'd spent forty years in academia. He'd read more books than most people will read in three lifetimes. And he was, by any equally measurable standard, one of the most rigid human beings I have ever encountered. Not because he was dumb. *Because* he was smart. His intelligence had become a power tool — and the only thing he'd learned to build with it was walls.

If intelligence protected you from rigidity, this man should have been the Dalai Lama in a sport coat. Instead, he was a cautionary tale with tenure.

The Smartest Person in the Room Problem

Here's the thing nobody tells you about being smart: it doesn't make you wise. It makes you *dangerous*.

I know. I know. We've spent our entire lives being told that intelligence is the golden ticket. That if you're smart enough, curious enough, well-read enough, degreed enough, you'll figure it out. You'll see through the nonsense. You'll think your way to clarity. Your IQ will be the lighthouse that guides you safely through the fog of aging and uncertainty and change.

Let me introduce you to a concept that is going to ruin your day: *motivated reasoning.*

Motivated reasoning is what happens when your brain uses its considerable horsepower not to find the *truth*, but to defend the *position it already holds*. And the more horsepower you have — the higher your IQ, the more educated you are, the more verbally skilled you are — the better you are at it. Smart people don't just have opinions. They have *arguments*. They have data. They have citations. They have that devastating conversational move where they reframe your point in a way that sounds like agreement but is actually a setup for demolition.

A person with an average IQ who's wrong about something will say, "I just think that's how it is." A person with a high IQ who's wrong about the same thing will say, "Well, if you look at the longitudinal data from the Brookings Institution, you'll see that the structural factors actually support my position when you control for..." — and forty-five minutes later, they're still wrong, but now everyone's too exhausted to argue.

Intelligence doesn't prevent rigidity. It *upgrades* it. It gives rigidity a tailored suit, a corner office, and an argument you can't beat — not because the argument is right, but because the person making it has spent a lifetime learning how to make wrong things sound right.

Your PhD is not a vaccine. It's a power tool. And like all power tools, it cuts in whatever direction you point it.

What Actually Predicts Wisdom

You're not going to like this part.

In 2025, researchers Shi, Liu, Xu, and Tang published a study in *Personality and Individual Differences* that should be required reading for every person who has ever confused being smart with being wise. They gave 612 participants validated measures of ambiguity tolerance, epistemic curiosity, wisdom (using the Abbreviated San Diego Wisdom Scale), and psychological well-being. Then they controlled for demographics and ran the numbers.

What predicted wisdom?

Not IQ. Not education. Not years of experience. Not the number of books you've read or degrees you've framed.

Ambiguity tolerance. Your ability to sit with unclear, uncertain, contradictory, or unresolved information without your nervous system treating it like a house fire.

And the mechanism was specific — almost beautiful in its simplicity. The data showed a sequential mediation chain: **ambiguity tolerance led to epistemic curiosity, which led to wisdom, which led to psychological well-being.** Four links in a chain, and the first one — the link that makes all the others possible — is your capacity to tolerate not-knowing.

Let me translate that into English so plain it hurts: when you can sit with "I don't know" without panicking, you become curious. When you're curious, you seek out diverse perspectives and deeper understanding. That seeking builds wisdom. And that wisdom — not certainty, not comfort, not "having all the answers" — is what actually makes you happy in the long run.

Now here's the killer: the chain only works if the first link holds. If you can't tolerate ambiguity — if "I don't know" feels like falling — you never become curious. If you're never curious, you never develop wisdom. If you never develop wisdom, the only well-being strategy you have left is *comfort*. And comfort, as we established in Chapter 1, is a shrinking room.

Your IQ is completely irrelevant to whether the first link holds. A person with an IQ of 100 who can say "I don't know" without flinching is on a better trajectory than a person with an IQ of 150 who treats uncertainty like a personal insult. The 150 will be more *articulate* about their rigidity. They'll defend it with better arguments. They'll be wrong more impressively. But they'll be wrong.

The Uncomfortable Truth: Intelligence doesn't make you wise. It makes you better at defending your existing beliefs against incoming evidence. The smarter you are, the more sophisticated your avoidance strategies become. You don't change the channel — you write a think piece about why the channel was wrong.

Research Spotlight: The Berlin Wisdom Paradigm

Starting in the early 1990s at the Max Planck Institute in Berlin, the late psychologist Paul Baltes and his colleague Ursula Staudinger developed one of the most ambitious research programs ever attempted on the topic of wisdom. They didn't just philosophize about what wisdom *was* — they built a way to *measure* it. Their framework defined wisdom as expert knowledge about the fundamental pragmatics of life: life planning, life management, and life review.

What Baltes and Staudinger found, again and again, surprised people. Neither personality alone nor intelligence alone predicted wisdom-related performance. What did? The *interface* between personality and intelligence — constructs like creativity, cognitive style, and the willingness to engage with complexity rather than reduce it. When they projected their wisdom measures into a space defined by thirty indicators of personality and intellectual functioning, wisdom retained a significant chunk of uniqueness. It was its own thing. Not "being smart" plus "being nice." Not "having experience" plus "being calm." A distinct capacity that lived in the gap between what a person knew and what they were willing to not-know.

In the most elite-performing participants — the ones who scored highest on wisdom — Baltes found something telling: many of them were clinical psychologists. Not because clinical psychologists are inherently wiser than anyone else, but because their professional lives required them to sit with ambiguity, complexity, and human contradiction *every single day*. Their job was, essentially, to tolerate not-knowing for a living. And that daily practice — not their IQ, not their training, not their degrees — was what built their wisdom.

The lesson: wisdom isn't earned in libraries. It's earned in the gap between certainty and uncertainty. And the only price of admission is your willingness to stay in that gap.

Let's do something uncomfortable. (Get used to that sentence. It's going to show up a lot.)

When was the last time you genuinely changed your mind about something important? Not something trivial — not "I switched to oat milk" or "I tried a different route to work." Something that *mattered*. A political position. A judgment about a person. A belief about how the world works. A long-held assumption about yourself.

If you can point to a specific moment in the last year — great. Hold onto that. You'll need it.

If you can't remember the last time… that's not a character flaw. That's data. And the data is telling you something about the ratio of intelligence to wisdom in your current operating system.

The Fortress of Logic

Let's talk about what intelligence actually *does* in a person who has low distress tolerance. Because it doesn't do nothing. It does something very specific, very impressive, and very destructive.

It builds fortresses.

A person with low distress tolerance and average intelligence handles uncomfortable information the same way a toddler handles broccoli: they push it away, make a face, and refuse to engage. It's not sophisticated. It's not convincing. Everyone can see what's happening.

A person with low distress tolerance and *high* intelligence does something much more subtle. They don't push the broccoli away — they construct a peer-reviewed argument for why broccoli is overrated, cite three nutritional studies that support their preferred alternative, invoke a philosophical framework about bodily autonomy and vegetable choice, and then pivot to a charming anecdote about their grandmother's cooking that makes everyone forget the broccoli was ever on the table.

The information was just as uncomfortable. The avoidance was just as complete. But the *mechanism* was so sophisticated that nobody noticed — least of all the person doing it.

This is the intelligence trap. Smart people don't avoid discomfort less than anyone else. They avoid it *better*. Their arguments are more polished. Their rationalizations are more convincing. Their intellectual frameworks are more elegant. And because their avoidance *looks* like engagement — because it uses the language and structure of critical thinking — they often fool themselves into believing they're being rigorous when they're actually being defensive.

The smartest person in the room is often the person with the most beautiful, impenetrable fortress. And they built it so well that they've forgotten there's a world outside the walls.

Exercise: The Evidence Threshold Test

Purpose: To reveal where your thinking has calcified by establishing (or discovering the absence of) a personal falsifiability standard for your strongest beliefs.

Instructions:

1. Get a piece of paper. Write down three opinions you hold strongly. Choose ones that generate heat — the kind where disagreement doesn't just feel *wrong*, it feels *personal*. These can be political, professional, ethical, spiritual, relational, whatever. The more strongly you hold them, the more useful this exercise becomes.

2. Under each opinion, answer this question in writing: **"What specific evidence would I need to see to change my mind about this?"**

Not "what would it take to weaken my position slightly." What would it take for you to say, "I was wrong. I've changed my mind." Be specific. What data? What experience? What argument from what source? Write it down.

3.   If the answer is "nothing could change my mind" — write that down too. Don't fudge it. Don't dress it up. If there is truly no evidence, no argument, no experience that could shift your position, that's important information.

4.   For each opinion, also answer: **"When was the last time I actively sought out information that contradicted this belief?"** Not stumbled across it. *Sought it out.* Deliberately. Intentionally. With the goal of understanding, not debunking.

What You Might Notice: Most people have at least one opinion where the answer to question 2 is either "nothing" or something so extreme it might as well be nothing ("I'd change my mind if someone proved, with a controlled experiment conducted by Jesus himself, that..."). That's a locked door. That's a belief you're holding not because the evidence supports it, but because *letting it go would cost you something.* Identity. Belonging. The feeling of certainty in an uncertain world.

And that cost — the emotional cost of being wrong — is what this whole book is about. The beliefs you can't let go of aren't your strongest beliefs. They're your most *protected* beliefs. And what they're protecting isn't truth. It's comfort.

You might also notice that question 4 is devastating. Most people, even very smart people, realize they haven't actively sought opposing evidence on their strongest beliefs in *years.* Maybe ever. They've encountered it accidentally and dismissed it. They've been challenged by it socially and defended against it. But sought it out? On purpose? With genuine curiosity? Almost never.

That's the trap. Intelligence without curiosity is just a faster engine with no steering wheel.

Debrief: The goal of this exercise isn't to abandon your beliefs. The goal is to hold them with *open hands* instead of clenched fists. A belief you've pressure-tested — one you've actively tried to break and found that it holds — is a hundred times stronger than one you've simply protected from challenge. The irony is that the only way to have truly strong beliefs is to be willing to let them go. If they survive the test, they're earned. If they don't, they were never yours to begin with — they were just comfortable furniture you never thought to move.

The Curiosity Dividend

I want to end this chapter with something that isn't depressing, because I've essentially spent three thousand words telling you that your intelligence is a liability and your strongest beliefs might be emotional security blankets with footnotes. That's a lot to sit with. (See what I did there? You're already practicing.)

Here's the upside: the intelligence trap has an escape hatch. And it's not complicated. It's not expensive. It doesn't require a retreat in Sedona or a second PhD.

The escape hatch is *curiosity*.

Not the performative kind — not "I'm curious about your perspective" said in the tone of voice that means "I'm about to explain why your perspective is wrong." Real curiosity. The kind that starts with "I don't know" and doesn't immediately try to fill the silence with an answer. The kind that asks questions it doesn't already have answers to. The kind that reads things that make it uncomfortable and doesn't stop reading just because the discomfort kicks in.

The 2025 ambiguity study found that the path from ambiguity tolerance to wisdom runs *through* curiosity. Not around it. Not over it. Through it. You have to be curious to become wise, and you have to tolerate not-knowing to become curious, and you have to tolerate emotional discomfort to tolerate not-knowing.

Intelligence is the engine. Curiosity is the steering wheel. And distress tolerance is the fuel.

You can have the most powerful engine on the planet. But if you've got no steering wheel and an empty tank, you're just a very expensive object sitting in a garage, going nowhere, making a lot of noise.

Chapter Takeaway: Intelligence is a power tool, not a compass. Without distress tolerance — specifically, the ability to tolerate the discomfort of being wrong — intelligence just makes you faster at building fortresses around positions you should have abandoned years ago. The escape hatch is curiosity, and curiosity requires the one thing intelligence can't provide: the willingness to say "I don't know" without your identity collapsing.

Your degree didn't make you wise. It made you really, really good at sounding wise while being exactly as stubborn as you were at 22 — just with better footnotes.

Chapter 3

The Stubbornness Muscle

Your brain has a gym for doing things you don't want to do. You should probably use it.

Somewhere in the middle of your brain — tucked between the two hemispheres, draped over a bundle of nerve fibers called the corpus callosum like a saddle over a very anatomically specific horse — there is a piece of neural real estate about the size of a large grape.

It doesn't look like much. In cross-section, it's a strip of cortex that most neuroscience textbooks used to gloss over on the way to sexier brain regions. It's not the amygdala, which got famous for fear. It's not the prefrontal cortex, which got famous for executive function and impulse control. It's not the hippocampus, which got famous for memory. For decades, this little strip of cortex was the neurological equivalent of a character actor — present in every scene, essential to the plot, but never on the poster.

Then the researchers got curious.

And what they found changed everything.

The structure is called the anterior midcingulate cortex. The aMCC. And it does something remarkable: it decides whether the hard thing in front of you — the thing you actively, viscerally, do-not-want-to-do — is worth doing anyway.

Not the easy thing. Not the fun thing. Not the thing you're already motivated to do because the reward is obvious and the effort is minimal. The *hard* thing. The thing every fiber of your being wants to walk away from. The conversation you want to leave. The question you don't want to ask. The belief you don't want to examine. The emotion you don't want to feel. The aMCC is the brain structure that lights up when you override your own resistance — when you tell the voice in your head that says "this is too hard, let's do something else" to sit down and shut up, because you're not done yet.

Here's the part that should make you sit up straight: this structure is trainable. It literally, physically grows when you use it. And it literally, physically shrinks when you don't.

Welcome to the most important gym you never knew you had a membership to.

The Tenacity Hub

Let me tell you about Lisa Feldman Barrett. She's a University Distinguished Professor of Psychology at Northeastern, she runs a lab at Massachusetts General Hospital, and she has one of those careers that makes other scientists mildly furious in that productive way that generates good research. In 2020, her team — Barrett along with Alexandra Touroutoglou, Joseph Andreano, and Bradford Dickerson — published a review in the journal *Cortex* that pulled together decades of evidence on the aMCC. The paper was called "The Tenacious Brain: How the Anterior Mid-Cingulate Contributes to Achieving Goals."

It's dense. It's technical. It's the kind of paper that uses the phrase "domain-general cost-benefit computation" unironically. But the core finding is breathtakingly simple: the aMCC is the brain's tenacity hub.

Stay with me here, because this is where it gets interesting.

The aMCC sits at the intersection of almost everything your brain does. It receives signals from systems involved in attention, reward processing, memory, emotion, sensory integration, and motor control. It is, in Barrett's words, one of the most *connected* structures in the entire brain. It's like the air traffic control tower for effort — constantly taking in data about what's happening inside you (how tired are you? how motivated? how scared?), what's happening outside you (how hard is this? how rewarding? how dangerous?), and making a real-time calculation about whether the effort is worth the cost.

When the aMCC calculates that the effort *is* worth it — even though it's hard, even though it hurts, even though you don't want to — you persist. You stay. You push through. You do the thing you don't want to do.

When the aMCC calculates that the effort *isn't* worth it — or when the aMCC itself is too weak or too atrophied to do the math properly — you quit. You leave. You reach for the easier option. You change the channel.

This is not a metaphor. This is neuroscience. Your ability to stay in the fire — literally, physically, neurologically — depends on the structural integrity of a specific piece of cortex that is measurable on an MRI.

Superagers and the Shrinking Brain

Now here's where this gets personal.

Most brains shrink as they age. That's not me being dramatic — it's cortical thinning, and it's one of the most well-documented phenomena in neuroscience. The cortex loses volume over time. Neural connections weaken. Processing speed declines. It's gradual, it's variable, and it's normal.

But there's a group of people — researchers call them "superagers" — for whom the normal rules don't quite apply. Superagers are typically eighty-plus-year-olds who perform on memory and cognitive tests at the level of people twenty to thirty years younger. Their brains don't look like the brains of other eighty-year-olds. In some regions, their brains look more like the brains of fifty-year-olds.

And guess which brain structure is consistently, measurably thicker in superagers compared to typical older adults?

The aMCC.

It's not the only difference — superagers tend to have more robust brain networks generally — but the aMCC finding is one of the most reliable. These people, who are aging cognitively at about half the rate of their peers, have kept their tenacity hub intact. They haven't let it atrophy. They haven't let the muscle thin.

On the other end of the spectrum — because there's always another end — you find the people who have lost the most aMCC volume. These tend to be people experiencing depression, apathy, and neurodegenerative diseases like Alzheimer's and Parkinson's. Conditions characterized by, among other things, a fundamental inability to generate the motivation to do difficult things. The aMCC isn't just smaller in these people. In some cases, it's functionally disconnected from the networks it's supposed to be integrating.

I'm not telling you this to scare you. (Okay, I'm telling you this to scare you a *little*.) I'm telling you this because the implication is extraordinary: the difference between cognitive superaging and cognitive decline may be — at least partially — a difference in how much you've trained the aMCC. A difference in how often you've done things you don't want to do.

The Uncomfortable Truth: There's a region in your brain that grows when you do things you hate and shrinks when you stop challenging yourself. It doesn't care whether the challenge is physical or emotional. And it doesn't give you credit for things that *used* to be hard but aren't anymore. The growth requires perpetual discomfort. Welcome to the gym that never closes.

If you've heard of the aMCC before, it's probably because of Andrew Huberman. The Stanford neuroscientist turned podcaster brought the aMCC into the mainstream in 2023 and 2024 through a series of episodes and a viral conversation with former Navy SEAL David Goggins. The message was compelling and shareable: there's a brain structure that grows when you do hard things. Cold showers. Extra reps. Running when you don't want to. Huberman even coined the term "micro-sucks" — small, chosen acts of discomfort that activate the aMCC and, theoretically, build your willpower over time.

It was great. It was viral. It got millions of people interested in a brain structure they'd never heard of. And it was incomplete.

Here's what Huberman emphasized: *physical* challenges. The extra set of squats. The cold plunge. The early morning run. These are legitimate aMCC activators. When you force yourself to do a physically demanding thing your body is screaming at you to stop doing, the aMCC lights up like a Christmas tree. No argument there.

Here's what Huberman *didn't* emphasize, and what this book is going to spend the next ten chapters hammering home: **the aMCC doesn't know the difference between physical effort and emotional effort.**

Let me say that again, because it's the most important sentence in this chapter: *the aMCC doesn't know the difference between physical effort and emotional effort.*

The cost-benefit calculation it runs — "Is this hard thing worth doing?" — doesn't distinguish between running another mile and staying in a hard conversation. Between adding weight to the barbell and questioning a belief that makes you feel safe. Between enduring cold water for three minutes and sitting with grief instead of numbing it with work, alcohol, screens, or certainty.

The aMCC responds to *resistance overcome.* That's it. That's the input. And the emotional resistances — the ones that challenge your identity, your worldview, your relationships, your deepest assumptions about who you are and how the world works — are, for most people, *far more difficult* than any physical challenge. Most of us would rather run a marathon in the rain than have an honest conversation about our marriage. We'd rather sit in an ice bath than sit with the uncertainty of not knowing whether we've been right about something we've been certain about for twenty years.

The cold shower is easy. The hot conversation is hard.

And the hot conversation is the one that determines whether you age into wisdom or rigidity.

Research Spotlight: The aMCC and the Cost of Comfort

Here's a detail from Barrett's research that should haunt you in the best possible way: the aMCC grows when you do things you don't want to do, but — and this is critical — *once you start wanting to do them, the growth effect diminishes.*

Read that again. Let it land.

The cold shower that terrified you in January? By March, when you've started to kind of enjoy it, your aMCC is getting less activation from it. The new exercise routine that was brutal in week one? By week six, when your body has adapted, the aMCC has largely moved on. It got its growth from the *resistance.* When the resistance faded, so did the growth stimulus.

This means the aMCC requires *perpetual novelty of discomfort.* You can't find one hard thing and do it forever and expect the muscle to keep growing. You have to keep finding *new* hard things. New challenges.

New areas of resistance. New forms of effort that your brain hasn't habituated to yet.

In the physical domain, this is straightforward — switch up your workout, try a new sport, learn a new skill. In the emotional domain, it's more complex and more powerful. There is an essentially *infinite* supply of emotional challenges available to any human being willing to look for them. Hard conversations you've been avoiding. Beliefs you've been protecting. Relationships you've been managing instead of engaging with honestly. Losses you've been numbing instead of feeling.

The aMCC never runs out of emotional material. The only limit is your willingness to use it.

The Mirror Moment

When was the last time you did something genuinely difficult — not routine-difficult, not "my schedule is packed" difficult, but *new*-difficult? Something that made you feel incompetent. Uncertain. Out of your depth. Something where you didn't already know how it was going to turn out.

I'm not talking about hard work. Most of us do hard work every day. I'm talking about hard *growth*. The kind where you're not applying a skill you already have to a problem you already understand, but where you're genuinely in over your head, uncertain of the outcome, and doing it anyway.

If it's been more than a month, your aMCC is quietly losing volume. No judgment. Just neuroscience. The muscle doesn't care about your intentions. It cares about your reps.

Let me paint a picture of what aMCC training looks like when you extend it beyond the physical and into the territory that actually determines how you age.

Physical aMCC workout: You add five minutes to your run when your body says stop. Your aMCC fires. Growth happens. Good.

Emotional aMCC workout: Your spouse says something that makes your blood pressure spike, and instead of snapping back, leaving the room, or going silent, you take a breath and say, "Tell me what you mean by that." Your aMCC fires. Growth happens. Better.

Cognitive aMCC workout: You read an article that contradicts a belief you've held for fifteen years, and instead of closing the tab, writing a snarky comment, or mentally debunking it sentence by sentence, you read the whole thing with the genuine question: "What if this person has a point?" Your aMCC fires. Growth happens. Best.

Existential aMCC workout: You sit alone in a quiet room with no screen, no book, no podcast, no music, and no plan, and you let whatever comes up — the anxiety, the grief, the boredom, the unnamed dread, the voice that says "what's the point?" — you let it exist without trying to make it stop. Your aMCC fires. Growth happens. Terrifying. Essential.

The cold shower is great. I'm not knocking the cold shower. But if the cold shower is the *only* hard thing you're doing — if you're toughing out the ice bath at 6 AM and then spending the rest of your day avoiding every emotional challenge life throws at you — you're training one arm and letting the other one atrophy. You're building physical tenacity and emotional fragility. You're getting very good at enduring cold water and very bad at enduring uncertainty.

The aMCC doesn't discriminate. But you have to feed it the right challenges if you want the right growth.

Exercise: The Emotional Gym Log

Purpose: To begin tracking *emotional* aMCC workouts — moments where you experienced emotional discomfort and had the option to stay or flee.

Instructions:

1. For the next seven days, keep a simple log. You can use a notebook, your phone, a sticky note on the fridge — whatever you'll actually use. Low friction is the goal here. We're building a habit, not a masterpiece.

2. Every evening, write down one moment from the day where you experienced emotional discomfort. This could be an argument. A challenging interaction. An uncomfortable thought. A moment of uncertainty. A flash of irritation. A wave of sadness you didn't want to feel. A conversation that made you want to leave. It doesn't have to be dramatic. Minor discomfort counts. Actually, minor discomfort is *better* for this exercise, because it's where most of the avoidance happens — the small, invisible, daily moments of "I'd rather not."

3. For each moment, note three things:

    -   **(a) What the discomfort was.** Name it. Be specific. "I felt defensive when my daughter told me I always do [thing]." "I felt anxious when I didn't know the answer to a question at work." "I felt irritated when someone disagreed with me on social media."

    -   **(b) Whether you stayed or fled.** "Stayed" means you sat with the feeling, engaged with the situation, let yourself experience the discomfort without immediately escaping it. "Fled" means you changed the subject, left the room, distracted yourself, went silent, got angry, doubled down on being right, reached for your phone, or deployed any other strategy to make the feeling stop.

- **(c) What it felt like in your body.** This is the one most people skip. Don't skip it. Emotions live in the body before they live in the mind. Tightness in the chest. Heat in the face. Clenched jaw. Stomach drop. Shallow breathing. Cold hands. The body's data is honest in a way the mind's data often isn't.

4. At the end of seven days, count your "stayed" entries and your "fled" entries.

What You Might Notice: Most people discover two things. First, they flee far more often than they realized. The escape responses are so fast, so automatic, so well-practiced that they happen below the level of conscious awareness. You're reaching for the phone before you even realize you were uncomfortable. You've changed the subject before you even register that the previous subject was painful. The avoidance is not a *choice* in any meaningful sense — it's a reflex. And you can't change a reflex you don't know you have.

Second, most people discover that the physical sensations of emotional discomfort are surprisingly *specific*. They're not vague. They're not "I felt bad." They're "There was a tightening behind my sternum that radiated up into my throat, and my hands got cold, and I had the impulse to stand up and leave." When you start noticing the physical signature of your discomfort, you develop an early warning system. You can feel the flee response *building* before it executes. And that microsecond of awareness — that tiny gap between "I notice I'm uncomfortable" and "I'm already distracted" — is the window where everything changes.

That's the rep. That's the growth. Right there. In the noticing.

Debrief: You don't need to stay in *every* uncomfortable moment. Some discomfort should be avoided. Toxic situations, abusive dynamics, genuine danger — flee from those. Please.

This book is not asking you to endure harm and call it growth. That's not wisdom. That's masochism with a reading list.

What we're targeting is the other kind — the survivable discomfort. The kind where the urge to flee is about *preference*, not safety. The kind where nothing bad will actually happen if you stay, but your nervous system is screaming at you to go anyway because it's been trained by decades of avoidance to treat mild emotional discomfort like a five-alarm fire.

Those moments — the survivable, non-dangerous, merely-uncomfortable moments — are the ones where the aMCC grows. Start noticing them. Start counting them. Start choosing, one rep at a time, to stay in a few of them a little longer than your body wants you to. That's the workout. That's the growth. That's the beginning of everything that follows.

What's Coming Next

We've established three things so far. First: aging concentrates you, and the default trajectory is toward rigidity (Chapter 1). Second: your intelligence can't save you from that trajectory and might actually accelerate it (Chapter 2). Third: there's a specific, trainable brain structure — the aMCC — that determines whether you persist through discomfort or collapse into avoidance, and its most important applications aren't physical but emotional (this chapter).

Now we need to talk about the fuel that's been powering your avoidance engine for decades. The thing that feels like clarity but works like a drug. The thing that feels like strength but functions like a cage.

We need to talk about certainty.

But that's Chapter 4. And you've done enough work for now. Go do your homework. One emotion. One log entry. One rep.

Chapter Takeaway: Your brain has a literal muscle for doing hard things — the anterior midcingulate cortex. It grows when you challenge yourself with things you don't want to do and shrinks when you stop. The most important exercises aren't physical — they're the emotional reps you do every time you stay in a moment you want to leave.

You want to grow this thing? Don't just add a mile to your run. Call your estranged sibling. Read the op-ed you hate. Sit in the room after the fight instead of leaving. That's the set that counts.

End of Part I, Chapters 1–3

The Discomfort Dividend — Humbolton Press Ken Konet, M.Ed., MBA -e

---

Chapter 4

The Certainty Narcotic

How being "right" became the most dangerous drug in old age.

I need you to think about the last time you were absolutely, bone-deep *certain* about something.

Not pretty sure. Not "I've looked into it." Not the kind of confident where you're open to hearing another side but feel reasonably grounded in your position. I mean *certain*. The kind of certain where someone pushing back on your view didn't feel like a conversation — it felt like an *assault*. Where the disagreement bypassed your intellect entirely and landed straight in your chest. Where you could feel your jaw tighten, your posture shift, your voice drop into that register that says *I will die on this hill and I will take you with me.*

Got it? Good. Hold that memory. Stay with the feeling.

Now I need you to consider the possibility — and I know this is going to be a tough sell, given that you've spent most of your adult life treating this feeling like a virtue — that that warm, righteous, unshakable certainty is the most dangerous thing happening in your brain.

Not the thing you were certain *about*. The certainty *itself.*

The belief might be perfectly valid. You might be right. That's not the point. The point is what certainty *does* to you neurologically, emotionally, and relationally when it stops being a conclusion you've arrived at through honest investigation and starts being a chemical you're using to regulate your emotional state. Because those are two very different things. And the distance between them is the distance between wisdom and rigidity.

Your Brain on "I Knew It"

Let's talk about what happens in your brain when you encounter information that confirms what you already believe. Because it's not subtle.

Your brain releases dopamine. Not a lot — this isn't the dopamine surge of a slot machine jackpot or your first kiss. It's a small, quiet pulse. A micro-reward. A little neurochemical pat on the back that says: *Good job. You were right. The world is exactly as you thought it was. Everything is in order.*

It feels like clarity. Like truth. Like the satisfying click of a puzzle piece dropping into place.

Now let's talk about what happens when you encounter information that *contradicts* what you already believe. Your amygdala — the brain's alarm system — fires. Not dramatically, not in a full-blown fight-or-flight response (usually), but enough to generate a signal that registers as *threat*. The contradictory information doesn't feel like a puzzle piece. It feels like someone just kicked the table and scattered the whole puzzle.

Your brain doesn't like that feeling. Nobody's brain likes that feeling. And your brain has developed an extraordinarily sophisticated set of tools for making that feeling stop. It can dismiss the information. It can attack the source. It can generate a counter-argument so fast you don't even realize it's happening. It can redirect your attention to something — anything — that restores the feeling of coherence. It can selectively remember the evidence that supports your position and conveniently forget the evidence that doesn't. It can do all of this in less time than it takes to blink.

This isn't a moral failing. This is motivated reasoning. It's the default operating system of every human brain on the planet. And in small doses, in the context of a life that regularly challenges you, it's manageable. It's just a cognitive bias — one of many — and you can compensate for it if you're aware of it.

But here's where it gets dangerous: the dopamine hit from "I was right" and the amygdala alarm from "I might be wrong" create a behavioral loop. Over time, without intervention, you start *seeking* the hit and *avoiding* the alarm. You curate your information diet for maximum confirmation and minimum challenge. You surround yourself with people who agree with you. You reach for certainty the way a smoker reaches for a cigarette — not because you need it for any rational purpose, but because it *regulates your emotional state.*

Certainty becomes a drug. And like all drugs, tolerance builds. What used to give you a hit of "I was right" at forty — reading a newspaper editorial you agreed with, having your position validated by a colleague — doesn't cut it at sixty. You need stronger doses. More extreme sources. Louder agreement. More dramatic dismissal of the other side. The needle moves. The dosage escalates. And before you know it, you're mainlining outrage at 7 AM just to feel something that resembles clarity.

That's not staying informed. That's using information as a narcotic.

The Uncomfortable Truth: Being right feels identical to being closed. The neurochemical signature of "I knew it!" is indistinguishable from the neurochemical signature of "I've stopped learning." If certainty has become your emotional regulation strategy, you're not getting wiser. You're getting high on your own confirmation bias.

In Chapter 3, I told you about the aMCC — the brain's tenacity hub that grows when you do things you don't want to do. Now I need to introduce you to another brain pattern, one that's just as important and far less famous. Neuroscientists call it the FADE pattern. It stands for Fronto-Amygdalar Age-Related Differences in Emotion. Which is a mouthful. But the concept is elegantly simple, and it might be the most important thing you learn in this book.

Here's what happens in the aging brain, documented through functional MRI studies by researchers including Peggy St. Jacques and Roberto Cabeza at Duke University: as you get older, the amygdala — your brain's reactive alarm system — becomes *less* active in response to negative emotional stimuli. At the same time, the prefrontal cortex — your brain's executive regulatory system — becomes *more* active.

On the surface, this sounds like great news. The reactive part of the brain is calming down. The thoughtful part is stepping up. Emotional regulation improves with age. The elderly are paragons of equanimity. Pop the champagne.

Except it's not that simple. Because there are two completely different reasons why the amygdala might be less active, and they produce completely different outcomes.

Scenario One: Regulation. The prefrontal cortex has genuinely learned, through years of practice, to modulate the amygdala's alarm signal. The negative information still gets *processed* — the person still feels it, acknowledges it, engages with it — but the prefrontal cortex provides context, nuance, and proportional response. This is emotional wisdom. This is what maturation looks like in the brain. This is the FADE pattern doing exactly what it's supposed to do.

Scenario Two: Suppression. The prefrontal cortex has learned to *suppress* the amygdala's alarm signal — not to modulate it, but to shut it down. The negative information doesn't get processed. It gets blocked. The person doesn't feel it because they've gotten so good at not-feeling that the signal barely registers anymore. This isn't regulation. This is avoidance at the neural level. The person isn't processing difficult emotions — they're filtering them out before they can land.

Same brain scan. Same FADE pattern. Two entirely different people.

In Scenario One, you get Ed from Chapter 1 — the person who can encounter hard things and hold them without breaking. In Scenario Two, you get Diane — the person who has constructed such an effective neural firewall against discomfort that nothing challenging gets through. She's not calm. She's *numb*. And the numbness looks like peace from the inside and feels like a wall from the outside.

The variable that determines which scenario you're living in? You guessed it. Distress tolerance. The person who has spent decades practicing the art of staying with difficult feelings has trained their prefrontal cortex for regulation. The person who has spent decades avoiding difficult feelings has trained their prefrontal cortex for suppression.

The FADE pattern is a fork, not a destination. And certainty — the relentless, escalating pursuit of being right — is the express lane to Scenario Two.

Research Spotlight: The Need for Cognitive Closure

In the 1990s, psychologists Arie Kruglanski and Donna Webster developed a construct called "need for cognitive closure" — the desire for a definite answer to a question, *any* answer, as opposed to ambiguity or uncertainty. High need for closure isn't about wanting truth. It's about wanting *resolution*. The click of the lock. The feeling that the question has been answered and you can stop thinking about it.

What Kruglanski and Webster found is unsettling in the context of aging: people high in need for closure tend to "seize" on early information (latching onto the first answer that reduces uncertainty, regardless of whether it's correct) and "freeze" on it (becoming resistant to new information once the closure has been achieved). They rely more heavily on stereotypes. They conform more readily to group opinion. They become more dogmatic. They show increased hostility toward people who disrupt their sense of certainty — not because those people are wrong, but because they *reopen the question.*

And here's the uncomfortable punchline: need for cognitive closure increases with stress, fatigue, cognitive load, and time pressure. All of which become more common as people age. The aging brain, unless deliberately counterbalanced, drifts toward closure. Toward certainty. Toward the comforting click of questions answered and cases closed.

This drift isn't pathological. It's efficient. The brain is conserving resources by reducing the number of open questions it has to maintain. But efficiency and wisdom are not the same thing. In fact, they're often opposites. Wisdom requires keeping questions open. Efficiency requires closing them. And the brain, left to its own devices, will choose efficiency every time.

Unless you train it to choose otherwise.

The Positivity Trap

Let me connect this to something we touched on in Chapter 1, because it's the other half of the certainty story.

Laura Carstensen's "positivity effect" — the documented tendency for older adults to preferentially attend to and remember positive information — is generally presented as a good thing. And in many ways it is. Who doesn't want to be happier? Who doesn't want to focus on what's good instead of what's bad? If older adults are naturally shifting toward a more positive emotional landscape, shouldn't we celebrate that?

Here's the problem: there is a meaningful difference between *choosing* to focus on the positive and *being unable to engage with the negative.* The first is selective attention. The second is a filter that removes uncomfortable data before it can be considered.

When the positivity effect operates through genuine regulation — when a person encounters negative information, processes it, and then *chooses* to direct their energy toward positive action or meaning — it's a superpower. It's the emotional equivalent of triage: I see all of it, I acknowledge all of it, and I'm going to focus my limited energy where it can do the most good.

When the positivity effect operates through avoidance — when a person filters out negative information before processing it, skips the articles that upset them, changes the channel when the news gets hard, dismisses the opinions that challenge their worldview — it's not selective attention. It's a blinder. And the person wearing the blinder feels great *inside* the blinder and has no idea that the world they're seeing is incomplete.

Certainty is the mortar that holds the blinder together. Every avoided challenge, every dismissed perspective, every moment of "I don't need to hear this" gets sealed in place with another layer of "I already know what I need to know." And gradually, imperceptibly, the blinder becomes a wall, and the wall becomes a room, and the room becomes the only world the person can see.

They feel certain. They feel right. They feel at peace. And they are trapped.

Let's do some quick math. Think about your media diet for the past week. All of it — news, social media, podcasts, videos, conversations, books.

How much of what you consumed *confirmed* what you already believed? Gave you that warm hum of "exactly" or "see, I told you"?

How much of it *challenged* you? Made you genuinely uncomfortable? Presented a perspective you found credible but disagreeable?

If the ratio is more than 80/20 in favor of confirmation, you're not staying informed. You're self-medicating. And the fact that your drug of choice comes in the form of "information" — that it *looks* like engagement, that it *feels* like critical thinking — makes it harder to recognize, not easier. The most dangerous addictions are the ones that look like virtue.

Exercise: The Certainty Inventory

Purpose: To map where certainty has become a coping mechanism rather than a conclusion — and to learn the difference between the two.

Instructions:

1. Write down five things you're "certain" about. Choose beliefs, opinions, or positions you'd defend strongly. Political, personal, spiritual, professional, relational — whatever generates the most heat. The more strongly you hold them, the more useful this exercise becomes.

2. For each one, answer honestly — and I mean honestly, not "honestly in a way that makes you feel good about yourself":

- **When did I become certain about this?** Give a rough year or life stage. Was it a gradual accumulation of evidence? A single transformative experience? Something you absorbed from your family, community, or media environment without much examination?

- **Have I actively engaged with a credible opposing viewpoint in the last 12 months?** Not stumbled across it and dismissed it. Not encountered it in a Facebook comment and rolled your eyes. *Engaged with it.* Read or listened to the best version of the opposing argument, from a credible source, with the genuine goal of understanding why a thoughtful person might hold that view.

- **If someone I respect deeply — someone whose character and judgment I admire — told me they held the exact opposite position, would my first impulse be curiosity or defensiveness?** Don't answer with what you *want* your impulse to be. Answer with what it *actually* would be. Feel it in your body.

- **Does this certainty make me feel *safe* or *right*?** These are different things. Safety is about emotional regulation — this belief reduces my anxiety about the world. Rightness is about identity — this belief tells me who I am. Both are valid motivations for holding a belief. But only one of them is about truth.

3. Now sort your five certainties into two categories: **conclusions** and **positions**. Conclusions are beliefs you arrived at through open investigation and would be willing to revise if compelling new evidence appeared. Positions are beliefs you adopted for emotional protection and would resist revising regardless of evidence.

What You Might Notice: Conclusions feel light. You hold them and you're willing to set them down. You can describe the evidence for them *and* the best evidence against them. You don't feel a spike of adrenaline when someone disagrees.

Positions feel *heavy*. You grip them. You defend them before anyone attacks them. You can describe the evidence for them in exhaustive detail but can barely articulate the strongest argument against them. When someone disagrees, you feel it in your chest before you feel it in your head.

The positions are the ones doing drug work for you. They're regulating your emotional state by providing a hit of certainty in an uncertain world. That doesn't make them wrong. Some positions might be factually correct. But you're not holding them because they're correct. You're holding them because they're *comfortable*. And the comfort is the trap.

Debrief: The goal isn't to become uncertain about everything. Radical uncertainty is paralysis, not wisdom. The goal is to know the *difference* between a conclusion and a position — and to be honest with yourself about which ones you're holding for epistemic reasons and which ones you're holding for emotional ones. A conclusion held with open hands is stronger than a position held with clenched fists, because the conclusion has been tested and the position has only been protected.

You might find that some of your positions, once examined, convert into conclusions — they hold up under scrutiny and you can articulate *why* with genuine intellectual honesty. Great. Those were never the problem. The problem is the ones that can't survive the examination. The ones that feel load-bearing. The ones where the question "what would change your mind?" produces a blank stare or a clenched jaw.

Those are your certainty narcotics. And the first step to recovery is the same as any other addiction: admit you're using.

I want to be clear about something before we move to Part II: I am not anti-certainty. That would be absurd. You need to be certain about some things. You need to be certain that cruelty is wrong and kindness matters and the people you love deserve your best effort. You need to be certain enough about your values to act on them. The world requires a functional relationship with certainty.

What the world does *not* require — what wisdom does *not* require — is certainty as a lifestyle. Certainty as a personality. Certainty as the air you breathe and the ground you stand on and the wall you build between yourself and everything that might change you.

The antidote to certainty-as-drug isn't doubt. It's *flexibility*. The ability to hold your beliefs firmly enough to act on them and loosely enough to revise them. To say "I believe this strongly, AND I'm open to being wrong." That "and" is doing the heaviest lifting in this entire book. Because most people use "but" — "I believe this strongly, BUT I'm open to being wrong" — and "but" negates everything that comes before it. "And" holds both truths simultaneously. That's the work. That's the aMCC workout. That's wisdom.

We'll get to the tools in Part II. For now, just sit with the question: Which of my certainties are conclusions, and which are narcotics?

Don't rush to answer it. The rushing is the problem.

Chapter Takeaway: Certainty is not strength. It's a narcotic — a way of regulating emotional discomfort by shutting down the input that causes it. The wiser path isn't to abandon your beliefs. It's to hold them with open hands, so new evidence can land instead of bouncing off. The brain wants closure. Wisdom requires keeping the case open.

Being right is cocaine for old people. The first hit is free. The rest costs you everything.

PART II: THE MECHANICS

The science and the skills

Chapter 5

Distress Tolerance 101

It's not about liking pain. It's about surviving it without running.

Let's get something out of the way right now: I am not asking you to enjoy suffering.

I'm not asking you to smile through pain. I'm not asking you to grit your teeth through grief and pretend it's building character. I'm not asking you to lean into discomfort like it's a trust fall and the universe will catch you. I have three master's degrees and not a single one of them taught me that misery is a gift. (Though one of them tried. The instructor wore a lot of hemp.)

I'm not promoting stoicism, which in its Instagram-repackaged form basically amounts to "don't have feelings." I'm not promoting masochism, which is a whole different section of the bookstore. And I'm absolutely not promoting that particular brand of toxic positivity that reframes every terrible experience as a "blessing in disguise" and tells you that the universe never gives you more than you can handle, which is statistically and morally insane.

What I *am* asking you to do — and this is the entire premise of this book compressed into a single request — is something far simpler and far harder than any of those:

The next time something hurts — emotionally, cognitively, socially, existentially — I'm asking you to *stay in the room.*

Not forever. Not happily. Not with a smile. Not without complaint. Just... stay. For ten seconds longer than your body tells you to leave. That's it. That's the whole game. Ten seconds of not-leaving when leaving is what every fiber of your nervous system is screaming at you to do.

Because that ten seconds? That micro-eternity between "I want to leave" and "I'm still here"?

That's where wisdom lives. Every bit of it.

What Distress Tolerance Actually Is (And What It Absolutely Isn't)

Psychologists have a clinical term for what we're talking about, and it has the unfortunate distinction of sounding both boring and intimidating at the same time: *distress tolerance*. It was formalized as a concept by Marsha Linehan as part of Dialectical Behavior Therapy (DBT) in the 1990s, and it has since been studied, measured, and validated across hundreds of clinical trials.

The definition is deceptively simple: distress tolerance is your perceived ability to withstand negative emotional or physical states.

That's it. It's not about *enjoying* negative states. It's not about *seeking them out*. It's about being able to be *present* during them — to feel the discomfort, acknowledge that it's happening, recognize that it won't kill you, and choose to stay with it long enough for something useful to happen. Something like processing. Something like learning. Something like growth.

Let me tell you what distress tolerance is not, because this is where most people get confused:

It's not toughness. Tough people endure. They white-knuckle. They grit. They survive by *refusing to feel*. Distress tolerance is the opposite — it's surviving by *choosing to feel*. By staying present with the discomfort instead of armoring against it. The tough person walls off the pain. The distress-tolerant person sits with it. The tough person comes out intact but unchanged.

The distress-tolerant person comes out changed — which is the whole point.

It's not stoicism. Modern pop-stoicism has been reduced to "don't let things bother you," which is essentially emotional suppression with a philosophy degree. Distress tolerance doesn't ask you to not be bothered. It asks you to *be bothered and stay anyway*. There's no pretending. No "it doesn't affect me." It affects you. You feel it. And you don't run.

It's not toxic positivity. "Everything happens for a reason!" is the battle cry of someone who cannot sit with meaninglessness. Distress tolerance doesn't require meaning. It doesn't require silver linings. It doesn't require that the pain was "worth it" or "happened for a purpose." It requires only one thing: that you stay present during it. Meaning might come later. It might not. That ambiguity? That's the workout.

It's not masochism. Let me be crystal clear: this book is not asking you to seek out pain, tolerate abuse, or endure harm. If a situation is genuinely dangerous — physically, emotionally, psychologically — get out. Distress tolerance is about the *survivable* discomfort. The kind that won't damage you but that your nervous system treats like a five-alarm fire because it's been trained by decades of avoidance to treat any discomfort as an emergency.

The difference between dangerous discomfort and survivable discomfort is critical, and most people have it completely backward. We avoid the survivable discomfort (the hard conversation, the challenging idea, the unfamiliar perspective, the uncomfortable silence) while tolerating the genuinely dangerous discomfort (the toxic job, the dead relationship, the unexamined belief that's slowly destroying our health). We run from conversations and stay in situations. We flee from feelings and endure circumstances.

Distress tolerance isn't about enduring everything. It's about staying with the *right* things — the things that are uncomfortable but survivable, challenging but not destructive, difficult but growthful.

The Uncomfortable Truth: Distress tolerance isn't about toughness. It's about *staying.* Tough people endure. Wise people stay. The difference is that endurance is about outlasting the pain. Staying is about being *present* with the pain long enough to learn from it. You can white-knuckle your way through a hard life and learn absolutely nothing.

The Escape Response: Faster Than You Think

Let me describe what happens in real time when a person with low distress tolerance encounters emotional discomfort. This happens in milliseconds. Most of it is below conscious awareness. And once you see it, you can't unsee it.

Millisecond 1–100: The signal arrives. Something happens. Your spouse says the thing. Your child rolls their eyes. The news anchor reports something that makes your stomach drop. A thought crosses your mind that you don't like. The signal enters your nervous system.

Millisecond 100–300: The body responds. Before your conscious mind has registered what happened, your body has already started reacting. Heart rate bumps. Shoulders tense. Breath shallows. Jaw tightens. Stomach clenches. These are not decisions. They're reflexes. Your autonomic nervous system has been doing this for a very long time, and it is *fast.*

Millisecond 300–500: The escape impulse fires. Your brain generates an escape strategy. Not deliberately — this isn't a calculated plan. It's a reflex, honed by decades of practice. The strategy might be anger (attack the source of discomfort so it stops). It might be distraction (reach for the phone, change the channel, start a different conversation). It might be intellectualization (analyze the situation until the feeling goes away). It might be humor (make a joke so nobody notices you're hurting). It might be shutdown (go numb, go quiet, disappear behind your eyes while your body stays in the room).

Millisecond 500–1000: The escape executes. You've already changed the subject. You've already picked up the phone. You've already launched the counter-argument. You've already left — mentally, if not physically. The discomfort has been avoided. The feeling has been short-circuited. And you probably didn't even notice it happening.

The entire sequence — from signal to escape — takes less than a second. It's not a choice. It's a *reflex*. And like all reflexes, it can only be changed through deliberate, repeated, conscious practice.

That's what the ten-second stay is for. It's not a technique. It's an *interruption*. You're inserting a ten-second pause into a thousand-millisecond process and saying: "Not yet. I'm going to feel this for ten more seconds before I decide what to do about it."

Ten seconds doesn't sound like much. But in the context of a sub-second escape response that has been running unchecked for decades, ten seconds is revolutionary. Ten seconds is the difference between reacting and responding. Between fleeing and staying. Between the old pattern and the new one.

Ten seconds is the rep.

If you're skeptical that distress tolerance is "trainable" — if some part of you suspects this is just how you're wired and there's not much to be done about it — I have 106 reasons to challenge that assumption.

A systematic review published in *Cognitive Therapy and Research* (2023) examined 106 studies on interventions for distress intolerance. The interventions ranged from mindfulness-based programs to Acceptance and Commitment Therapy (ACT) to Dialectical Behavior Therapy (DBT) to standard cognitive-behavioral approaches. The review asked two questions: Do these interventions reduce distress intolerance? And do the reductions predict meaningful changes in psychological flexibility?

The answer to both questions was yes. Consistently. Across multiple methodologies, populations, and intervention types.

Multiple approaches worked. The specific technique mattered less than the underlying principle: every effective intervention taught people, in one way or another, to *stay with discomfort instead of fleeing from it*. The modality varied. The mechanism was the same.

And the reductions stuck. They weren't temporary spikes. They predicted lasting improvements in psychological flexibility — the ability to adapt to changing circumstances, hold difficult emotions without being overwhelmed by them, and pursue valued actions even in the presence of discomfort.

In plain English: your ability to tolerate discomfort is not a fixed trait carved into your personality at birth. It's a skill. It can be taught. It can be practiced. It can be improved. At any age. You are not stuck with the distress tolerance you have right now.

Read that last sentence again. It's the most important sentence in this chapter.

I want to pause here and address something you might be thinking: "Okay, distress tolerance sounds important, but isn't this a therapy concept? Isn't this for people with anxiety disorders and borderline personality and addiction?"

Fair question. And the answer is: it *started* in clinical settings, yes. Linehan developed distress tolerance as a core DBT module for people whose emotional dysregulation was so severe it was threatening their lives. In that context, it's a clinical intervention. No argument.

But here's what the clinical literature has been slowly, grudgingly acknowledging for the past decade: low distress tolerance isn't just a clinical problem. It's a *human* problem. And it becomes a *bigger* human problem as you age, for three reasons that have nothing to do with pathology and everything to do with math.

First, the opportunities for avoidance multiply. When you're twenty-five, you can't avoid discomfort. Your boss makes you do things you don't want to do. Your roommate forces you to negotiate space. Your bank account forces you to tolerate uncertainty. You have no choice but to sit with discomfort because you don't have the resources or the authority to escape it. By fifty-five, you've accumulated resources, authority, routine, and — crucially — a social environment you've curated specifically to minimize challenge. The more control you have over your life, the easier it is to arrange that life so nothing uncomfortable gets through. And the easier it is to avoid discomfort, the more your distress tolerance atrophies — silently, invisibly, like a muscle you stopped using because you bought an elevator.

Second, the stakes of avoidance increase. When you avoid discomfort at twenty-five, you miss a growth opportunity. Inconvenient but recoverable. When you avoid discomfort at fifty-five, you miss a *last* growth opportunity. The windows are closing. The experiences that could have changed you are becoming less frequent. Every avoided conversation, every unfelt grief, every unexamined belief carries more weight because there are fewer remaining chances to revisit them.

Third, the compound interest kicks in. We covered this in Chapter 1, but it bears repeating in this context: avoidance compounds. Every time you escape a moment of discomfort, the escape response gets faster and the tolerance threshold gets lower. By midlife, the avoidance machinery is *so efficient* that many people don't even recognize it as avoidance anymore. It just feels like "knowing yourself." Like "having preferences." Like "being set in your ways." It feels like identity. But it's not identity. It's a reflex — a very fast, very practiced reflex that has been running without conscious oversight for decades.

Distress tolerance isn't a clinical intervention you need because something is wrong with you. It's a *life skill* you need because the default trajectory of the second half of life — more control, more comfort, more routine, less challenge — produces exactly the conditions under which distress tolerance atrophies most rapidly.

You are not broken. You are not diagnosable. You are just living in a world that makes avoidance very, very easy — and nobody told you that easy is the most dangerous thing your psychological health can be.

The Mirror Moment

Right now, in this moment — not hypothetically, not abstractly, but right now — there is something in your life you're avoiding thinking about.

A conversation you need to have. A question you need to ask. A decision you need to make. A feeling you need to feel. A truth you need to face. You know what it is. You just felt it. It flickered across your consciousness like a fish breaking the surface of a pond — visible for a moment, then gone.

Don't chase it. Don't try to solve it. Don't strategize about when you'll deal with it. Just notice that it's there. Acknowledge its existence without engaging with its content. You don't have to do anything about it right now.

You just have to not pretend it doesn't exist.

That's distress tolerance. Right there. In the noticing without fleeing. In the acknowledging without fixing. In the staying present with the knowledge that something is unresolved without grabbing for a resolution.

You just did a rep. Didn't even feel it, did you?

Exercise: The 10-Second Stay

Purpose: To build the foundational distress tolerance micro-skill — inserting a ten-second pause before the automatic escape response executes.

Instructions:

1. Choose one day this week as your practice day. Just one. We're not building a monastery. We're doing a pilot program.

2. Throughout the day, notice moments of emotional discomfort. They're everywhere once you start looking. Irritation when the barista gets your order wrong. Anxiety when an email sits unopened. Frustration when your spouse does the thing. Boredom when you're stuck in traffic. Sadness that shows up uninvited while you're folding laundry. Uncertainty about something you thought you'd decided. These don't have to be dramatic. The lower the stakes, the better — we're practicing fundamentals, not competing in the Olympics.

3. When you notice a moment of discomfort, do this: **Stay for ten seconds.** Don't fix it. Don't distract from it. Don't explain it away. Don't reach for your phone. Don't

change the subject. Don't launch a counter-argument.
Just notice what you're feeling. Where you feel it in your
body. What the impulse to escape feels like.

Count to ten if you need to. Slowly. Like you're defusing
a bomb. Because in a way, you are.

4. After ten seconds, you can do whatever you were going
    to do anyway. Leave. Distract. Fix. Argue. Whatever. The
    exercise is the ten seconds, not the outcome. We're not
    trying to change what happens after. We're trying to
    change the space *before*.

5. At the end of the day, write down: How many times did
    you practice the 10-Second Stay? What did you notice?
    What was harder than expected? What happened
    during the ten seconds?

What You Might Notice: Ten seconds is simultaneously
nothing and everything. In the context of a normal day, it's
barely perceptible. In the context of an active escape response,
it's an *eternity*.

Most people discover that their escape response is much faster
than they realized. They're reaching for the phone at second
two. They've changed the subject by second four. They're
mentally composing a rebuttal by second six. The ten seconds
exposes just how quickly and automatically the avoidance
machinery kicks in — machinery they didn't even know was
running.

Some people find the ten seconds genuinely difficult. Not
because anything bad happens during them — nothing bad
happens; that's kind of the point — but because the discomfort
of *not escaping* is its own kind of discomfort. You're so used to
the escape that the absence of the escape feels worse than the
original trigger. That's the dependency talking. That's the reflex
protesting its interruption. That's normal.

Debrief: You just completed your first deliberate rep of
distress tolerance. That's not a metaphor. You literally,

physiologically exercised the neural infrastructure we've been talking about for four chapters. The ten seconds of staying — uncomfortable, present, un-fixed, un-fled — is the micro-dose of the discomfort dividend.

And it compounds. Ten seconds today. Ten seconds tomorrow. Twenty seconds next week. A full minute by the end of the month. Each rep makes the next rep slightly easier — not because the discomfort diminishes (it doesn't, necessarily), but because the *relationship* to the discomfort changes. It stops being an emergency and starts being a sensation. Starts being *information*. Starts being something you can be curious about instead of something you have to flee from.

That shift — from "this discomfort is an emergency" to "this discomfort is information" — is the single most important psychological shift you will ever make. And it starts with ten seconds.

Chapter Takeaway: Distress tolerance isn't toughness, stoicism, or masochism. It's the simple, brutal, trainable skill of staying present during discomfort instead of running from it. 106 studies confirm it can be developed at any age. And it starts with the smallest possible unit of staying: ten seconds.

Nobody is asking you to enjoy the fire. We're asking you to stop leaving the room every time it gets warm.

Chapter 6

The Ambiguity Frontier

Learning to survive — and maybe even love — "I don't know."

I want you to try something. Read the following sentence slowly. Don't skim. Let each word land.

It's possible that the thing you've believed most strongly for the past twenty years is wrong, and you may never know for sure either way.

Now notice what happened in your body.

Did you feel that? That little lurch? That micro-twitch of resistance, like your brain hit a speed bump? Maybe a tightening in your chest. Maybe a flash of "well, that doesn't apply to me." Maybe an impulse — quick, almost subliminal — to argue with the sentence before you'd even finished reading it.

That's your ambiguity tolerance talking. Or rather, your ambiguity *intolerance* talking. And the speed and intensity of that reaction — how fast it showed up, how physical it felt, how quickly your brain generated a counter-argument — is one of the most important pieces of data about your psychological trajectory that you will ever encounter.

Because here's the thing about ambiguity: it is the natural habitat of wisdom. Wisdom doesn't live in the land of the certain. It lives in the territory of "I'm not sure." Of "it depends." Of "I can see both sides." Of "I used to think I knew, but now I'm not so sure." Every wise person in every tradition — philosophical, spiritual, clinical, or folk — has some version

72

of the same foundational capacity: they can hold uncertainty without collapsing.

And that sentence I asked you to read? If it made you want to skip ahead to a chapter with more concrete answers, you are exactly the person who needs to stay right here.

The Cognitive Cousin

In the last chapter, I introduced distress tolerance — the ability to stay present during *emotional* discomfort. Ambiguity tolerance is its cognitive cousin. Same family, different specialization. If distress tolerance is about staying in the room when the feelings get hard, ambiguity tolerance is about staying in the room when the *answers* aren't there.

And it's about more than just "being okay with uncertainty" in some vague, wellness-poster kind of way. Ambiguity tolerance has been studied rigorously since the 1940s, starting with Else Frenkel-Brunswik's work on authoritarian personality types and continuing through decades of research connecting it to creativity, decision-making, interpersonal flexibility, and — this is the part that should make your ears perk up — wisdom.

Let me give you the clearest, most recent data point, because it's the one that anchors this entire chapter.

In 2025, a research team led by Shi, Liu, Xu, and Tang published a study in *Personality and Individual Differences* that tracked the relationship between ambiguity tolerance and psychological well-being across 612 participants. They used the Multiple Stimulus Types Ambiguity Tolerance-II scale, the Epistemic Curiosity Scale, the Abbreviated San Diego Wisdom Scale, and a validated measure of psychological well-being. After controlling for demographics, they found a sequential mediation chain so clean it practically sparkles:

Ambiguity tolerance → Epistemic curiosity → Wisdom → Psychological well-being.

Four links. A chain. And the mechanism is elegant in its logic: when you can tolerate not-knowing, you become curious. When you're curious, you seek out diverse perspectives, new information, deeper understanding. That seeking — that active, curiosity-driven engagement with complexity — builds wisdom. And wisdom, in turn, predicts well-being. Not happiness exactly — well-being. The deeper, more durable kind that doesn't depend on things going well.

The chain only works if the first link holds. Break it — remove the ambiguity tolerance — and everything downstream collapses. No tolerance for uncertainty means no curiosity. No curiosity means no wisdom. No wisdom means the only well-being strategy you have left is comfort. And comfort, as we've now established across four chapters, is a shrinking room with very nice wallpaper and a lock on the inside.

The Uncomfortable Truth: Certainty is a closed door. Ambiguity is an open one. The person who "knows" has stopped learning. The person who can tolerate not-knowing is the person whose world keeps expanding. Here's the great irony: the person who says "I don't know" ends up knowing far more than the person who never says it.

Why "I Don't Know" Feels Like Falling

Let's talk about why ambiguity is so hard. Because it's not a character flaw to struggle with it. It's a *design feature* of the human brain.

Your brain is a prediction machine. That's its primary job — not thinking, not reasoning, not philosophizing. *Predicting.* From the moment you wake up to the moment you fall asleep, your brain is running a continuous simulation of what's going to happen next, based on everything that's happened before. When the prediction matches reality, the brain is satisfied.

Efficient. Calm. When the prediction *doesn't* match reality — when something unexpected, ambiguous, or contradictory shows up — the brain generates an error signal. An alarm. A "something is wrong" notification that demands attention and resolution.

Ambiguity is a *permanent* error signal. It's the brain encountering a situation where it can't generate a confident prediction — where the data is contradictory, the outcome is uncertain, and the "right answer" doesn't exist or can't be determined. And the brain *hates* this. Not mildly dislikes. *Hates.* The way a smoke detector hates smoke. It's not a preference. It's a built-in alarm system that screams for resolution.

This is why certainty feels so good. Certainty *resolves the alarm*. It shuts off the smoke detector. It tells the prediction machine, "It's okay, we've figured it out, you can stand down." The relief you feel when you arrive at certainty isn't intellectual satisfaction. It's *alarm cessation*. Your nervous system literally calms down.

And this is why "I don't know" feels like falling. It's the alarm staying on. It's the prediction machine running without a prediction. It's cognitive free-fall — the brain reaching for solid ground and finding nothing.

Most people will do almost anything to stop that feeling. They'll grab the first answer that presents itself, regardless of quality. They'll adopt someone else's certainty wholesale rather than sit with their own uncertainty. They'll dismiss complex information and embrace simple narratives. They'll attack the messenger who brought the ambiguity. They'll retreat into dogma, tribalism, or willful ignorance — not because they're bad people, but because the alarm is *unbearable* and these strategies make it stop.

Training ambiguity tolerance isn't about enjoying free-fall. It's about learning that free-fall won't kill you. That the alarm, while unpleasant, is not an emergency. That you can sit with an unanswered question for ten minutes, ten hours, ten days —

and not only survive, but discover things you never would have found if you'd grabbed the first available certainty and held on for dear life.

Research Spotlight: The Ambiguity–Wisdom Pipeline

Let's unpack the 2025 Shi et al. study more carefully, because the mechanism it reveals is worth understanding.

The researchers surveyed 612 college students (an important limitation — these aren't older adults, which means the findings need replication across age groups, but the theoretical model is robust). They measured ambiguity tolerance using a scale that captures reactions to unfamiliarity, complexity, uncertainty, and contradictory information. They measured epistemic curiosity — specifically "interest-type" curiosity, the kind driven by the pleasure of learning rather than the anxiety of not-knowing. They measured wisdom using the Abbreviated San Diego Wisdom Scale, which captures prosocial attitudes, emotional regulation, decisiveness, social advising ability, self-reflection, and tolerance for divergent values. And they measured overall psychological well-being.

What they found, after controlling for gender and grade level: ambiguity tolerance didn't just *correlate* with well-being. It *predicted* it — through a specific, sequential mechanism. First, ambiguity tolerance activated interest-type curiosity (if you can sit with not-knowing, you become *interested* in the not-known). Then, curiosity predicted wisdom (the seeking and exploring builds actual wise judgment). Then, wisdom predicted well-being (not because wise people have better lives, but because they have better *relationships with* their lives).

The sequential nature is crucial. You can't skip links. You can't go straight from ambiguity tolerance to wisdom without the curiosity. You can't go straight from curiosity to well-being without the wisdom. The chain has to run in order. And if the first link — ambiguity tolerance — is missing, none of the downstream benefits appear.

The implication for aging is stark: if you want to be well in your later years — not just comfortable, but *well* — you need to cultivate the ability to sit with "I don't know." Not as a one-time act of intellectual humility, but as a *practice*. A daily, repeated, deliberately uncomfortable practice.

The Mirror Moment

Here's a question I want you to carry with you after you read it. Don't answer it. Just carry it.

What's the question you're most afraid to ask — not because the answer would be dangerous, but because you might not be able to find the answer?

Not "what if I have cancer?" That's a fear question with a medical answer. I'm talking about the questions without clean answers. "Am I living the life I actually want?" "Have I been wrong about something fundamental?" "What if the people I've dismissed actually had a point?" "What would be left of my identity if I let go of [this belief/this role/this story about myself]?"

Sit with the question. Feel the itch to answer it. Notice how badly your brain wants resolution — wants to grab an answer, any answer, and make the alarm stop.

Don't let it. For now, just carry the question. We'll come back to it.

Not all ambiguity is created equal. And understanding *which* types of not-knowing hit you hardest is essential to training your tolerance for them. Through my work as an instructional designer and through the research on ambiguity tolerance, I've noticed that ambiguity comes in five distinct flavors — and most people have one or two that are significantly harder for them than the others.

Intellectual ambiguity. "I don't know the answer to this question." For some people, this is unbearable. The idea that there's a question out there they can't answer — especially in their area of expertise — triggers an almost primal anxiety. These are the people who Google everything mid-conversation, who can't let a debate end without establishing who was right, who mistake information for wisdom because at least information is *certain*.

Moral ambiguity. "I don't know if this is right or wrong." This is the one that gets people at 3 AM. The decisions that don't have a clean ethical answer. The situations where reasonable people disagree and nobody is clearly the villain. The recognition that you might have done something harmful despite having good intentions. People with low tolerance for moral ambiguity tend to become increasingly black-and-white in their thinking as they age — not because the world gets simpler, but because their capacity to hold complexity gets smaller.

Relational ambiguity. "I don't know where I stand with this person." Do they like me? Are they angry? Was that comment passive-aggressive or just awkward? Is this friendship genuine or transactional? Relational ambiguity is particularly cruel because it's essentially permanent — you can never fully know what another person thinks or feels, and every relationship involves a degree of not-knowing that has to be tolerated indefinitely.

Existential ambiguity. "I don't know what any of this means." The big ones. What happens when you die. Whether your life mattered. Whether you made the right choices. Whether there's a purpose or just a sequence. People with low existential ambiguity tolerance tend to gravitate toward rigid frameworks — religious, political, philosophical — not because the frameworks are true, but because they provide the architecture of meaning that the ambiguity threatens to dissolve.

Identity ambiguity. "I don't know who I am anymore." This one hits hardest in midlife, when roles shift, bodies change, and the story you've been telling about yourself stops matching the reality you're living. Am I still the person I was? Am I who I thought I'd become? What's left when the labels are stripped away? Identity ambiguity is the most destabilizing because it threatens the foundation — not just what you *think*, but who you *are*.

Here's why this taxonomy matters: most people can tolerate three or four of these just fine. It's the one or two that they *can't* tolerate that drive the rigidity. The intellectual whiz who can handle any factual uncertainty but falls apart when a relationship is ambiguous. The morally certain crusader who can't sit with ethical complexity. The person who has their identity locked down so tight that any challenge to their self-concept feels like an existential threat.

Your ambiguity tolerance isn't uniform. It has a shape. And knowing the shape tells you where your workout needs to happen.

Exercise: The Open Question Experiment

Purpose: To practice holding ambiguity deliberately — carrying an unresolved question without trying to close it.

Instructions:

1. Choose a question you genuinely don't know the answer to. Not a factual question with a Google-able answer. A real, open, messy human question. Examples:

    - "Am I in the right career — or am I just comfortable?"
    - "What actually matters at the end of a life?"
    - "Is this friendship still serving both of us, or am I keeping it alive out of habit?"
    - "Is there a version of this political issue where the other side has a legitimate point?"
    - "What would I do differently if I weren't afraid?"

2. Write the question on a card, a sticky note, or a piece of tape. Put it somewhere you'll see it every day — bathroom mirror, desk, dashboard, refrigerator, nightstand. Somewhere you can't avoid it.

3. For seven days, **do not try to answer the question.** This is the hard part. Every time you notice it, let the question exist. Observe the urge to resolve it. Notice whether your brain immediately starts generating answers — quick, confident, closure-oriented answers designed to make the uncertainty stop. Watch the answers float by. Don't grab them.

4. If you catch yourself trying to resolve the question — talking about it with a friend to get validation, Googling related topics, mentally constructing a framework — notice that impulse. It's not wrong. It's just the alarm sounding. The smoke detector going off because there's smoke, not fire.

5. At the end of seven days, write one paragraph about the experience. What was it like to carry the question? Did the question change over the week? Did your *relationship with* the question change? Did any new questions emerge from it?

What You Might Notice: Most people experience a physical urge to resolve the question. It feels like an itch you can't scratch. The brain *hates* open loops. There's actually a name for this — the Zeigarnik effect — the psychological tendency for incomplete tasks to occupy mental bandwidth until they're resolved. Your brain will keep returning to the question, nudging you, pestering you, offering quick answers, trying to close the loop.

Sitting with the open question — without resolving it, without abandoning it — is an act of cognitive courage. You are deliberately keeping the smoke detector on. You are choosing to live with the alarm instead of pulling the battery. And you are discovering, in the process, that the alarm is uncomfortable but not dangerous. That you can function, and think, and live, with an unanswered question humming in the background.

If you did this for seven days, you just trained your ambiguity tolerance more deliberately than most people do in a decade. And you might have noticed something unexpected: by day five or six, the question started to *deepen*. Not resolve — deepen. It became richer, more textured, more interesting. That deepening is the curiosity link activating. That's the wisdom pipeline starting to flow.

Debrief: Wisdom isn't knowing. Wisdom is not-knowing with grace. The question isn't whether you have answers — of course you have answers, you've been accumulating them for decades. The question is whether you can tolerate the moments when your answers aren't enough. When reality is more complex than your framework. When the honest response is "I don't know yet" and you let that "yet" hang in the air without grabbing for a conclusion.

That's the frontier. That's where wisdom lives. And the price of admission is ten seconds of staying — followed by seven days of carrying — followed by a lifetime of holding questions and answers simultaneously, with open hands, without needing either one to be final.

Chapter Takeaway: Ambiguity tolerance is the cognitive cousin of distress tolerance — and it's the first link in a chain that leads from uncertainty to curiosity to wisdom to well-being. The brain is designed to close open loops. Wisdom requires keeping them open. The skill is trainable. The discomfort is real. The dividend is everything.

"I don't know." Try saying it at Thanksgiving. Watch what happens. If people look at you like you've admitted to a crime, you've found your workout.

Chapter 7

The Fork in the Road

Why the decade between 45 and 55 decides everything.

There's a decade in your life — and if you're reading this book, there's a very good chance you're either in it, approaching it, or looking at it in the rearview mirror — where everything converges.

Your parents start dying. Or they die. Suddenly, or slowly, or in that agonizing space between where they're here but they're not here, and you spend your weekends in hospitals and assisted living facilities and on the phone with siblings you haven't talked to in months, and you feel things you didn't know you could feel, and nobody prepared you for any of it.

Your kids leave. Or they don't leave, which is its own kind of crisis. Or they leave and come back. Or they leave and become people you don't entirely recognize — people with lives and opinions and relationships that don't include you as a central character anymore. And you feel the absence like a phantom limb.

Your body starts sending memos you can't ignore. The knee. The back. The blood pressure. The thing the doctor wants to "keep an eye on." The reading glasses you swore you'd never need. The morning where getting out of bed requires negotiation with muscles that used to just *do what they were told*.

Your career either reaches a peak — and you realize the view from the top isn't what you imagined — or reveals itself as a plateau, and you realize you might be standing on the highest ground you're ever going to reach.

And somewhere in the middle of all this — between the funeral arrangements and the empty nest and the MRI results and the performance review that felt a lot like a participation trophy — a question starts tapping on the inside of your skull. Quietly at first. Then louder. Then incessantly.

Is this who I'm going to be for the rest of my life?

That question, if you let yourself hear it, is the fork in the road. And the decade in which it appears — roughly 45 to 55, give or take — is the most psychologically plastic period of your adult life since adolescence. More malleable than your twenties, when you were too busy building to notice what you were building with. More flexible than your thirties, when you were too invested in the scaffolding to question the blueprint.

In this decade, everything is up for grabs. Not because you choose it — nobody chooses this level of disruption — but because life strips away the distractions and leaves you standing in front of a mirror you can't dim. And what you do with what you see in that mirror — whether you process it or avoid it, explore it or close it, grieve it or wall it off — determines the entire trajectory of your remaining years.

Left goes to wisdom. Right goes to rigidity. And there are no road signs.

The Catalyst Theory

Judith Glück and Susan Bluck have spent their careers asking a question that most of us avoid: why do some people become wiser through life's difficulties while most people don't?

Not "why do some people have harder lives" — the research is clear that adversity alone doesn't produce wisdom. Plenty of people survive terrible things and come out the other side not wiser but *harder*. More defended. More rigid. More certain that the world is hostile and the only sensible response is to build higher walls.

No, Glück and Bluck were asking something more precise: given that *everyone* encounters difficulty, what determines whether that difficulty becomes a catalyst for growth or an accelerant for entrenchment?

Their answer is the MORE Life Experience Model, and it's the most complete framework for understanding wisdom development that exists in psychology. The model identifies five psychological resources that determine whether adversity produces wisdom or rigidity:

Managing uncertainty and uncontrollability. Not "controlling the uncontrollable" — that's a fantasy. Managing the *feeling* of uncontrollability. Accepting that you can't determine the outcome while still engaging with the process. The wise person says, "I don't know how this will turn out, and I'm going to do my best anyway." The rigid person says, "I need to know how this will turn out or I'm not playing."

Openness to new experiences, perspectives, and people. Not the Instagram version of openness (travel photos and fusion cuisine). Real openness. The willingness to encounter an idea that threatens your framework and sit with it instead of dismissing it. The willingness to have your mind changed. The willingness to be *wrong* in public.

Reflectivity — specifically, exploratory reflection. This is the distinction that matters most. Reflective people think about their experiences. But there are two kinds of reflection, and they produce completely different outcomes. *Closure reflection* says, "That was hard, I survived, time to move on." It seeks resolution. Endpoint. Done. *Exploratory reflection* says, "That was hard. What does it mean? What did it teach me? How did it change me? What don't I understand yet?" It seeks *meaning*. And meaning, unlike closure, doesn't have an endpoint. It keeps unfolding.

Emotional sensitivity and emotion regulation. Notice these are *both* listed — not one or the other. Wise people feel deeply *and* manage what they feel. They don't suppress. They don't explode. They hold. They let the wave come and they stay standing. That dual capacity — to be moved and to not be wrecked — is the emotional signature of wisdom.

Midlife is the crucible in which these resources are either activated or abandoned. The convergent pressures of the 45–55 decade — loss, transition, physical decline, existential reckoning — create conditions that *demand* these resources. And the people who have them, or who develop them under pressure, come through the crucible wiser. The people who don't have them, or who refuse to develop them, come through the crucible more rigid.

Same fire. Different metals. Different results.

The Uncomfortable Truth: Grief is not an obstacle to wisdom. It's the *admission price*. If you haven't grieved something real — a person, a dream, a version of yourself that no longer exists — you haven't paid the cover charge. And if you *have* grieved but processed it through closure instead of exploration — "I'm over it" instead of "what did it teach me?" — you paid the cover charge but stayed in the lobby.

Grief: The Master Class

Let's talk about the elephant in the midlife room. Because grief is not a side topic in this conversation. It's the *main* topic.

Between 45 and 55, most people encounter loss at a scale they've never experienced before. Not all at once, usually. In waves. A parent. A marriage. A career identity. A physical capacity. A friendship that quietly expires. A version of yourself that you realize, one morning, no longer exists — the young version, the version with options, the version who could still become anything.

These losses are not optional. They are not avoidable. They are the tuition for being alive past a certain age. And what you do with them — how you process them, whether you process them — is the single most consequential decision of your middle years.

Grief properly processed is the most powerful distress tolerance training program in human experience. Nothing else comes close. Because grief asks you to do the hardest thing a human being can do: sit with irreversible loss. Not fix it. Not undo it. Not find the silver lining or the lesson or the meaning. Just *sit with the fact that something you loved is gone and it's never coming back.*

If you can do that — if you can stay present with loss, feel the full weight of it, let it change the shape of your inner world without collapsing or hardening — you have earned your distress tolerance Ph.D. You have proven, to yourself and to your nervous system, that the worst feeling in the world is survivable. That ambiguity — the ultimate ambiguity, the one about what comes after loss — doesn't have to be resolved to be tolerated.

Grief properly processed teaches you that you can feel devastated and grateful in the same breath. That the world can be unfair and beautiful at the same time. That you can lose someone and still be whole. These are not ideas. They are *experiences.* And they only come from staying with the grief long enough for the grief to teach them to you.

Grief *avoided*, on the other hand, is the most powerful accelerant of rigidity in human experience. The loss you won't feel becomes the wall you build. And every subsequent loss — every challenge, every change, every disruption — gets added to the wall because the original grief was never processed and there's nowhere else for the pain to go.

The person who has avoided their grief is the person who can't tolerate anyone else's. The person who has walled off their own sadness is the person who gets angry when the world tries to make them feel something. The person who has "moved on" without actually moving *through* is the person whose world keeps shrinking, because every reminder of loss has to be avoided, and the list of reminders keeps growing.

You cannot get wise without getting grieved first. And you cannot get grieved by "moving on." You can only get grieved by moving *through*.

Research Spotlight: Hard-Earned Wisdom

Nic Weststrate, Michel Ferrari, and Monika Ardelt (2016) published a study on what they called "hard-earned wisdom" — and the name is deliberate. The wisdom is not given. It's not inherited. It's not stumbled upon. It's *earned*. Through work. Through pain. Through the specific, deliberate, deeply uncomfortable act of sitting with hard experiences and letting them change you.

Their key finding: wiser individuals process life challenges through *exploratory processing*. They seek meaning and growth from adversity, even when the process is painful, slow, and doesn't arrive at neat conclusions. They ask, "What is this teaching me?" — and they tolerate the possibility that the answer might be "I don't know yet" for weeks, months, or years.

Less wise individuals process the same challenges through *closure processing*. They try to put the experience behind them as quickly as possible. "It is what it is." "Everything happens for a reason." "I need to move on." These are the mantras of closure processing, and while they provide immediate relief, they produce no growth. The pain stops, but the lesson never arrives.

Critically, both groups *experienced* difficult things. The variable wasn't adversity. Everyone gets adversity. The variable was *what they did with it.* And what the wise ones did was stay. Stayed uncomfortable. Stayed curious. Stayed open to the possibility that the experience was changing them in ways they hadn't figured out yet.

The suffering is not the point. The staying is.

Separately, longitudinal research from Wink and Helson (1997) tracked individuals from early adulthood into later life and found that psychological mindedness and openness measured in the twenties and thirties positively predicted wisdom decades later. The people who develop wisdom at 65 were asking hard questions at 30. The seeds are planted decades before the harvest. Which means, if you're in the 45–55 window right now, the seeds you planted in your younger years are about to bear fruit. The question is whether you'll eat the fruit or let it rot because it doesn't taste like what you expected.

The Ego Question

There's one more piece of the midlife fork that we need to talk about, and it's the one nobody wants to talk about, so naturally we're going to talk about it right now.

Every wisdom tradition in human history — every single one, across every culture, every century, every philosophical and spiritual lineage — says the same thing about the relationship between ego and wisdom: the wiser the person, the smaller the ego.

Not the weaker the ego. The *smaller* the ego. There's a difference. A weak ego can't hold a position, can't tolerate criticism, can't function under pressure. A small ego can do all of those things — but it doesn't need to be the loudest thing in the room while it does them. A small ego doesn't require constant validation, doesn't need to win every argument, doesn't feel threatened by someone else's competence, doesn't interpret disagreement as attack. It has *room*. Room for other people's perspectives. Room for complexity. Room for the possibility that it might be wrong.

A large ego, by contrast, takes up all the space. It needs to be right. It needs to be acknowledged. It needs to be the main character. And as people age, the ego faces a series of threats that are, to put it mildly, destabilizing: your body is declining, your professional relevance may be diminishing, your children don't need you the way they used to, the world is changing in ways that don't center you, younger people are making decisions about the future that you won't live to see.

These threats can go one of two ways. They can *shrink* the ego — expanding the person's awareness beyond themselves, softening the need for control, deepening the capacity for humility and awe. Or they can *inflate* the ego — producing a defensive, compensatory grandiosity that manifests as increased rigidity, dismissiveness, and the need to assert authority in every interaction.

Ed and Diane again. Same threats. Different responses. Ed let the threats shrink his ego — he became more curious, more humble, more interested in other people's experiences because his own ego didn't need to be the center of every conversation. Diane let the threats inflate hers — she became more defensive, more dismissive, more certain, because the alternative was to sit with the terrifying possibility that the world was moving on without her.

The ego question isn't separate from the distress tolerance question. It *is* the distress tolerance question. The ego shrinks when you can tolerate the discomfort of not being the most important person in the room. It inflates when you can't.

The Mirror Moment

This one's going to sting. That's the point.

If you're in the 45–55 window: What loss are you currently carrying that you haven't fully processed? Not the loss you've "dealt with." The one you've *managed*. The one you've put in a box and labeled "handled" but that still sends up flares when you least expect it — the tightness when the song comes on, the irritability at the holidays, the strange anger that appears when someone mentions a subject that shouldn't be charged but is. What are you "moving on from" that you haven't actually moved *through*?

If you're past 55: Looking back at the midlife decade, what loss did you process through closure instead of exploration? What wall did it build? And is the wall still there?

Exercise: The Grief Inventory

Purpose: To identify unprocessed losses that may be contributing to rigidity — not to retraumatize, but to notice where the walls are.

Instructions:

1. List the three most significant losses you've experienced in the past ten years. These don't have to be deaths — though they can be. Losses of roles, relationships, identities, abilities, dreams, and illusions all count. The loss of "the way things were supposed to go" counts. The loss of a version of yourself counts.

2. For each loss, answer three questions:

   - **Did I process this through exploration or closure?** Exploration sounds like: "I'm still making sense of this." "It changed how I see things." "I learned something about myself I didn't expect." Closure sounds like: "That chapter is behind me." "I've dealt with it." "It is what it is." "I don't think about it anymore."

- **What emotion is still attached to this loss that I haven't fully felt?** Not the emotion I *did* feel — the one I *didn't*. The anger underneath the sadness. The relief underneath the guilt. The fear underneath the acceptance. The loneliness underneath the "I'm fine." There's almost always a feeling beneath the feeling, and the one underneath is usually the one that got avoided.

- **Did this loss change my view of anything — myself, others, the world — or did I return to the same view I had before?** If the loss changed your worldview, even uncomfortably, that's a sign of exploratory processing. If your worldview snapped back to exactly what it was before — same beliefs, same assumptions, same framework, as if the loss never happened — that's a sign of closure processing. The experience was survived but not metabolized.

3. Look at your answers. The losses you processed through closure, that didn't change your worldview, and that still carry unfelt emotions — those are the ones most likely to be building walls rather than building wisdom. They're the unprocessed material of your midlife. And they're still doing work — not the work of growth, but the work of rigidity.

What You Might Notice: This exercise might feel heavier than the previous ones. That's by design. We've been building toward this. The first six chapters were foundation. This is the floor where the weight lands.

Some of you will feel something reading those three questions that surprises you. A catch in the throat. A heat behind the eyes. A tightness that wasn't there thirty seconds ago. That feeling — that unexpected, uninvited, unwelcome surge of *something* — is the unprocessed material making itself known. It's been waiting. It's patient. It doesn't go away because you stop looking at it. It just goes quiet — and quiet, in the world of unprocessed grief, is not the same as gone.

If you need to put the book down and come back, that's not quitting. That's distress tolerance in action. You're staying with the discomfort of the exercise by giving yourself a break *without abandoning the work*. That's the difference. The person who puts the book down and comes back tomorrow is doing the work. The person who puts the book down and never comes back is doing the avoidance. You know which one you are. Come back.

Debrief: The fork in the road doesn't close. This is the single most important thing I can tell you about the midlife pivot, and I need you to hear it even if you're reading this at 70: it's not too late.

If you're past 55 and you recognize — sitting here, right now, with this inventory in front of you — that you went right instead of left. That you processed through closure. That you built walls instead of bridges. That the losses you didn't grieve have been quietly calcifying into the rigidity you feel in your opinions, your relationships, your body, your life — you are not too late.

The fork is still there. It's always there. The road doesn't disappear because you chose the wrong branch. You can walk back. You can find the fork again. You can take the other path. The only time it's genuinely too late is when you decide it is.

And deciding it's too late is, itself, a form of avoidance.

Chapter Takeaway: The decade between 45 and 55 is a window of extraordinary psychological plasticity. Grief, properly processed, is the most powerful wisdom-building experience in human life. The person who walks through midlife loss with open hands, an ego willing to shrink, and a willingness to explore instead of close walks out the other side wise. Everyone else walks out rigid. But the fork doesn't close. It never closes.

Somewhere between your first funeral where you're not the youngest person there and your first morning where your body audibly protests getting out of bed, you'll hit the fork. There's no GPS. There's only whether you learned to sit with the thing that hurts.

End of Chapters 4–7

The Discomfort Dividend — Humbolton Press Ken Konet, M.Ed., MBA -e

---

Chapter 8

The Social Wall

How rigidity kills your relationships — and how loneliness kills everything else.

Let me describe someone and you tell me if you recognize them.

They haven't made a genuine new friend in at least a decade. Their social world has contracted to two categories: family (obligation) and a small circle of people who agree with them about virtually everything (comfort). They have strong opinions about "kids today" — their music, their politics, their work ethic, their attention spans, their incomprehensible relationship with technology — and they haven't had a substantive, curious, mutually respectful conversation with someone under forty since their own children were young. When they encounter someone who thinks differently, their first impulse isn't curiosity. It's correction. Or dismissal. Or that particular conversational maneuver where they smile patiently while radiating a frequency that says *I'm waiting for you to finish being wrong so I can explain how things actually work.*

They're not lonely. Ask them and they'll tell you so. They have people. They have their spouse, their bridge club, their golf foursome, their book group where everyone reads the same genre and agrees about the same themes and nobody ever recommends anything that might disturb the afternoon. They have a full calendar. A busy life.

But busy and connected are not the same thing. Full and rich are not the same thing. And the difference between "not lonely" and "not isolated" is the difference between a room with furniture and a room with windows.

Sound familiar? Maybe it's a parent. Maybe it's a neighbor. Maybe it's the person who shows up at every holiday dinner and makes the room slightly smaller just by being in it.

Maybe — and I'm going to need you to stay with me here — maybe it's you.

The Fortress That Feels Like a Home

Social rigidity is one of those concepts that sounds like it describes other people. Rigid people. Difficult people. People who aren't like *you*. But social rigidity isn't about being difficult. It's about being *inflexible* — specifically, inflexible in how you engage with other people. And inflexibility, as we've established across seven chapters, doesn't announce itself. It creeps. It accumulates. It disguises itself as preference, discernment, self-knowledge, and the hard-earned right to spend your time however you damn well please.

A study published in the *Canadian Journal on Aging* examined social rigidity in older adults and found that the inability to adapt how you engage with other people was significantly linked to poorer life adjustment across multiple domains. Not cognitive rigidity — *social* rigidity. The inability to shift your interpersonal style based on context. The insistence on engaging with everyone the same way — your way — regardless of who they are, what they need, or what the situation calls for.

The person who lectures their adult children the same way they lecture their employees. The person who corrects their grandson's grammar at Thanksgiving. The person who cannot sit in a room with someone who voted differently without turning the evening into a tribunal. These aren't personality quirks. They're social rigidity. And they predict, with uncomfortable statistical confidence, a decline in life satisfaction, social support, and overall adjustment as the years pass.

But here's the finding that matters most: social rigidity *responded to intervention*. It wasn't permanent. It wasn't hardwired. It was a pattern — a deeply practiced, heavily reinforced, emotionally defended pattern — but a pattern nonetheless. And patterns can be changed.

The wall can come down. But only if the person inside it recognizes it's a wall and not a home.

The Uncomfortable Truth: The loneliest people in the world don't think they're lonely. They think they're *selective*. They think the problem is everyone else — too loud, too different, too young, too liberal, too conservative, too emotional, too soft. The wall they built to keep uncomfortable people out is the same wall keeping wisdom from getting in.

The Curating Trap

Let me complicate this with some nuance, because I know what you're thinking: "But I *should* be selective about who I spend time with. That's not rigidity — that's healthy boundaries."

You're right. Partially. And the partial rightness is what makes this so dangerous.

Laura Carstensen's socioemotional selectivity theory — which we've visited several times now — tells us that as people age and perceive their remaining time as limited, they naturally narrow their social circles to prioritize emotionally meaningful relationships. They spend less time with acquaintances and more time with people who matter to them. They let go of relationships that drain without enriching. This is adaptive. This is healthy. This is one of the genuine benefits of aging.

But there's a line. And the line is this: **Are you narrowing your social world toward meaning, or are you narrowing it toward agreement?**

Curating toward meaning looks like: "I want to spend my time with people who challenge me, enrich me, and share my values — even if they don't share all my opinions." It's selective but expansive. The circle is smaller, but the conversations within it are bigger.

Curating toward agreement looks like: "I want to spend my time with people who don't make me uncomfortable." It's selective and *contractive*. The circle is smaller, and the conversations within it are an echo.

The difference between these two is distress tolerance. The person who curates toward meaning can tolerate the discomfort of disagreement within a close relationship. The person who curates toward agreement can't. And over time — over decades — the agreement-curator's world doesn't just narrow. It *calcifies*. Every relationship becomes a mirror instead of a window. Every conversation confirms instead of challenges. Every person in the room shares the same perspective, the same language, the same assumptions. And the person at the center of this carefully constructed echo chamber feels *great*. They feel understood. They feel validated. They feel at peace.

They are also, by any meaningful psychological measure, trapped.

The Loneliness Data

Let me hit you with a number that should scare you more than anything else in this book.

Julianne Holt-Lunstad and her colleagues published a meta-analysis in 2015 that examined the relationship between social isolation, loneliness, and mortality. What they found: chronic social isolation carries a mortality risk equivalent to smoking fifteen cigarettes a day. It's more dangerous than obesity. More dangerous than physical inactivity. More dangerous than air pollution. Social isolation doesn't just make you sad. It *kills* you. Measurably. Statistically. Replicably.

And here's the cruel twist: social rigidity produces isolation without producing *the feeling* of isolation. The person inside the fortress doesn't feel alone. They feel surrounded — by family, by their curated circle, by their media diet of confirming voices. The isolation is structural, not experiential. They've walled themselves off from the kinds of social engagement that challenge, surprise, discomfit, and grow them — and they don't feel the absence because they don't know what they're missing.

You can be surrounded by people and still be socially isolated, if every person in your circle is a reflection of you. Diversity of perspective isn't a luxury. It's a survival mechanism.

The Intergenerational Workout

Here's where I'm going to make a specific recommendation that will probably make some of you roll your eyes, and I'm okay with that because eye-rolling is a mild form of discomfort and we've established that mild discomfort is where the growth happens.

Talk to young people. Genuinely. Not to educate them. Not to correct them. Not to share the wisdom of your years. To *learn from them.*

I know. I know. "What could they possibly teach me?" is the sentence that is already forming behind your eyes, and I need you to notice that that sentence — that reflexive dismissal of an entire demographic's capacity to contribute to your understanding — is social rigidity wearing a blazer.

Intergenerational conversation is a wisdom workout because it forces you into every kind of ambiguity simultaneously. You're encountering a worldview you didn't form. Language you don't use. Priorities you don't share. Cultural references you don't recognize. And you have to sit there, in the role of *learner* —

which, when you're the older person, requires a specific and deliberate shrinking of the ego that most people over fifty find genuinely difficult.

The discomfort of not being the expert in the room. The discomfort of not understanding the reference. The discomfort of having your assumptions challenged by someone with less life experience but a completely different vantage point. That's the workout. Every bit of it.

The Mirror Moment

Count the number of genuinely new relationships you've developed in the past five years. Not acquaintances — not the barista who knows your order, not the neighbor you wave to. People you've actually gotten to know. People who are different from you in some meaningful way — age, background, viewpoint, experience, life stage.

If the number is zero, that's not a lifestyle preference. That's data. And the data is telling you that your social world has stopped expanding and started contracting. Not because there aren't new people worth knowing — there are always new people worth knowing — but because the discomfort of engaging with someone unfamiliar has gradually exceeded your willingness to tolerate it.

Exercise: The Conversation Bridge

Purpose: To practice social flexibility by deliberately engaging with someone outside your comfort zone — not to change their mind or share your wisdom, but to *understand their experience.*

Instructions:

1. This week, have a genuine conversation with someone who is at least fifteen years younger or older than you. Not a transaction. Not small talk. A *conversation* — the

kind where you ask questions and listen to the answers with the same attention you'd give to someone you're trying to learn from. Because you are.

2. Ask them about their life. Their concerns. Their hopes. What they're excited about. What they're worried about. What they wish people your age understood about their experience. Don't offer advice. Don't correct. Don't relate everything back to your own experience. Don't begin sentences with "Well, in my day…" Just listen.

3. While listening, notice what comes up for you internally. Irritation? Judgment? Curiosity? Dismissal? Warmth? Discomfort? Superiority? Surprise? All of the above? Don't judge the reactions — just notice them. They're data about the shape of your social rigidity.

4. Afterward, write down: What did I learn that genuinely surprised me? Where did I feel the strongest urge to correct, dismiss, or redirect? What would happen if I had this kind of conversation once a week?

What You Might Notice: The hardest part isn't having the conversation. It's not *steering* it. The impulse to teach, correct, advise, compare, and redirect is overwhelming — especially when you're the older person. Decades of accumulated experience generate a constant internal commentary of "I know better," and keeping that commentary internal while someone tells you something you disagree with or don't understand is an aMCC workout of the highest order. The discomfort is the growth. If it felt easy, you weren't doing it right.

Debrief: One conversation won't tear down a wall. But it might crack a window. And a window is all you need to remember that there's a world out there that your fortress has been blocking. The goal isn't to become best friends with your barista's roommate. The goal is to prove to your nervous system that unfamiliar people, unfamiliar perspectives, and unfamiliar experiences are survivable — and that surviving them is how you grow.

Chapter Takeaway: Social rigidity is the loneliness trap that doesn't feel like loneliness — it feels like standards, preferences, and "knowing who you are." But when your social world only includes people who agree with you, you're not curating. You're hiding. And the wall you've built isn't protecting you. It's imprisoning you.

You know what the opposite of wisdom looks like? A 68-year-old who hasn't made a new friend in 15 years and thinks the problem is everybody else. That's not independence. That's a fortress with no windows.

PART III: THE PRACTICE

Where to do the work

Chapter 9

Sitting in the Fire

A field guide to practicing discomfort where it actually lives.

Okay. We've done the science. We've done the theory. We've built the vocabulary. You know what the aMCC is. You know about FADE and the positivity effect. You understand that ambiguity tolerance predicts wisdom and certainty is cocaine for the aging brain. You know that social rigidity will brick you into a fortress and grief will either crack you open or weld you shut.

Now comes the part where you actually have to do something uncomfortable.

I know. I'm sorry. Sort of.

Because here's the thing — distress tolerance isn't built by reading about distress tolerance. If it were, therapists would be the wisest people on the planet, and let me tell you, I've met some therapists who would disprove that theory in about six minutes. It's built in the specific, repeated, unglamorous moments where you choose to *stay* instead of *leave*. Not in a meditation retreat in the mountains. Not in a therapist's office on a Tuesday at 3 PM. At your kitchen table. In front of your news feed. In the mirror when your body reminds you it has an expiration date. In the silence when there's nothing left to distract you from the sound of your own unprocessed life.

These are the four arenas where the fire burns. And this chapter is your field guide for walking into each one without burning down.

The family dinner. The holiday gathering. The phone call with the sibling you love but can't talk to for more than twelve minutes without someone's voice getting tight. The moment your spouse says *the thing* — the thing they've been saying for twenty years, the thing that triggers the same response every single time, the response so automatic you can feel your body shift before your brain even registers what was said.

These are the highest-stakes, lowest-escape distress tolerance challenges in most people's lives. Because you can't fire your family. (Well, technically you can. But the exit interview is brutal and there's no severance package.)

The primary enemy at the kitchen table is the **urge to fix**. Someone shares a problem, a frustration, a feeling — and before they've finished the sentence, your brain is already assembling a solution. It's already drafting the email, scheduling the call, devising the plan. "Have you tried...?" "What you should do is..." "When I was your age..."

The fix-it reflex feels like helpfulness. It feels like care. It feels like *doing something*. But it isn't any of those things. It's avoidance. The fix-it reflex is your brain saying: *This person's discomfort is making ME uncomfortable. The fastest way to make MY discomfort stop is to solve THEIR problem so THEY stop being upset so I can stop feeling this feeling.*

You're not fixing their problem. You're fixing *your discomfort*. And the cost is that they never feel heard, you never feel the difficult emotion, and the relationship stays exactly where it is — functional, managed, and shallow.

The wise response is to stay with their discomfort without trying to make it go away. To listen without solving. To hold space without filling it. To say, "That sounds really hard," and *mean it*, and *stop talking*.

Exercise: The Kitchen Table Stay

Purpose: To practice staying in a family interaction that triggers your fix-it or flee response.

Instructions: 1. Choose one family interaction this week where you anticipate tension or discomfort. 2. Before the interaction, set a private intention: *I'm going to stay for ten seconds longer than I want to. I'm not going to fix, advise, correct, or leave until I've sat with whatever comes up.* 3. During the interaction, when the discomfort hits — notice it. Name it internally. ("This is frustration." "This is helplessness." "This is the urge to fix.") Notice where it lives in your body. Don't act on it for ten seconds. 4. After the interaction, write one sentence: What did I notice when I stayed?

Arena 2: The News Feed

Your media consumption is either a distress tolerance workout or a certainty IV drip. There is no neutral position. Every piece of media you consume either challenges you or confirms you, and you know which one your feed is mostly doing.

Here's a test: scroll through whatever you consumed yesterday — the articles you read, the podcasts you listened to, the social media posts you engaged with, the news programs you watched. Count the ones that confirmed what you already believed. Now count the ones that genuinely challenged you. If the ratio is more than 80/20 in favor of confirmation, you're not staying informed. You're self-medicating with agreement.

Reading things you agree with is not engagement. It's emotional regulation through confirmation — a dopamine drip of rightness that masquerades as critical thinking. And like all drips, you don't notice how dependent you've become until someone threatens to disconnect the line. Try going one week consuming *only* content from sources you'd normally dismiss. Just try. Watch how your body responds. The anxiety. The irritation. The creeping certainty that you're being *contaminated* by bad ideas. That's not intellectual discernment. That's withdrawal symptoms.

Reading things that genuinely challenge you — not the straw-man version of the other side, not the dumbest person making the weakest argument, but the *best* version of the argument you disagree with — is one of the most accessible aMCC exercises available to any human being with an internet connection.

Exercise: The Ideological Cross-Training Protocol

Purpose: To practice cognitive distress tolerance by deliberately engaging with high-quality content that contradicts your existing beliefs.

Instructions: 1. Identify one issue you feel strongly about — political, social, cultural. 2. Find the strongest, most well-argued, most *credible* version of the opposing position. Not a tweet. Not a meme. Not the worst person on the worst platform making the worst version of the argument. An article, essay, or book by someone who is thoughtful, educated, and genuinely holds the opposing view. 3. Read the entire thing. No skimming. No hate-reading. Read it the way you'd read something you agree with — looking for what's valid, what's interesting, what you hadn't considered. 4. After reading, write: (a) One point they made that I hadn't considered. (b) One thing I still disagree with but can articulate *why* without dismissing the person. (c) Did this change my view, even slightly? If not, did it deepen my understanding of *why* I hold my view?

Arena 3: The Body's Betrayal

Your body is going to decline. This is not pessimism. This is physiology. Your knees will creak. Your back will file formal complaints. Your eyes will negotiate for better contracts. Something will hurt that didn't used to hurt, and you will face a choice that plays out a hundred times between fifty and eighty: catastrophize ("This is the beginning of the end"), deny ("I'm fine, nothing's wrong"), or *stay* ("This is uncomfortable. I can be with this discomfort without it meaning I'm dying and without pretending it isn't happening").

The body is the most underrated distress tolerance training ground in human experience because it is always available and it is always honest. Your mind lies to you constantly — rationalization, minimization, intellectualization, denial. Your body doesn't know how to do any of that. It just reports. *There is pain here. There is tension here. There is fatigue here.* The body's data is pure signal. No spin. No narrative. Just sensation.

Learning to sit with physical discomfort — without dramatizing it, without denying it, without turning it into a story about aging or mortality or unfairness — is a direct, daily, inexhaustible distress tolerance workout.

Exercise: The Body Check-In

Purpose: To practice staying present with physical discomfort without catastrophizing or denying.

Instructions: 1. Sit quietly for three minutes. No screen, no music, no distraction. 2. Scan your body from head to feet. Notice every area of discomfort — tension, ache, stiffness, fatigue, pain. 3. For each area, resist the urge to label it ("That's my bad knee") or story it ("This is getting worse"). Instead, just describe the *sensation*: "There is tightness here." "There is a dull ache here." "There is heat here." 4. Stay with each sensation for thirty seconds without moving, adjusting, or fixing. 5. Notice: Does the sensation change when you stop resisting it?

Arena 4: The Silence Test

Can you sit in a room alone for twenty minutes without a screen, a book, a podcast, a conversation, or any form of external stimulation?

If the answer is "no" — or "why would I want to?" — that's not a comfort preference. That's a distress tolerance deficit. And the deficit isn't about silence. It's about what the silence *reveals*. Because the silence is a mirror. When you remove every external input — every screen, every voice, every distraction — what's left is *you*. Your thoughts. Your feelings. Your unprocessed material. The things you've been using all that noise to avoid.

Boredom will show up. Anxiety will show up. Grief might show up. Regret might show up. Existential dread — that low-frequency hum of *what is any of this for?* — might show up. And the impulse to reach for your phone will be almost unbearable, because your phone is the world's most sophisticated avoidance device and you've been training with it for over a decade.

Stay anyway. Whatever shows up is the material. The material is the workout.

Exercise: The 20-Minute Silence

Purpose: To practice being alone with your own thoughts and feelings without external regulation.

Instructions: 1. Set a timer for twenty minutes. Sit in a room alone. No phone. No book. No music. No TV. No writing. No meditation app. Just you and whatever shows up. 2. Notice what your mind does. It will resist. It will tell you this is pointless. It will generate to-do lists, urgent tasks, phantom itches, and very compelling reasons why you need to check your phone *right now*. 3. Stay anyway. For twenty minutes, your only job is to be present with whatever arrives. 4. When the timer goes off, write one paragraph: What came up? What thoughts? What feelings? What was the hardest moment? What surprised you?

Of the four arenas — kitchen table, news feed, body, silence — which one scares you the most?

Not which one is hardest intellectually. Which one makes your stomach clench when you imagine doing it? The one where you just thought, "I could probably skip that one."

That's your arena. The one you want to skip is the one you most need to enter. The avoidance is telling you exactly where the work is. Your resistance is a map, and the X is right where it's most uncomfortable.

The Uncomfortable Truth: You don't build distress tolerance in the gym, the meditation retreat, or the therapist's office (though all three help). You build it at the kitchen table when your spouse says the thing. In front of your news feed when the article makes your blood boil. In your aging body when the knee protests. And in the silence when there's nothing left between you and yourself. Those four arenas are the gym. You've had a membership your whole life. You just haven't been showing up.

Chapter Takeaway: Distress tolerance is built in four arenas: relationships (the kitchen table), cognition (the news feed), physical reality (the body), and self-confrontation (the silence). You don't have to master all four at once. Pick one. Start there. Ten seconds of staying is worth more than a year of reading about staying.

Here's your homework: tonight at dinner, when the thing happens that makes your blood pressure spike, don't respond for ten seconds. Feel the heat. Notice the urge. And then just... don't. Stay in the fire. See what happens when you stop trying to put it out.

Chapter 10

The Softened Edge

What actually changes in your nervous system when you stop fighting reality.

You know those people.

The ones who walk into a room and something shifts. Not dramatically — it's not charisma in the traditional sense, not the magnetic pull of someone who demands attention. It's subtler. More like a change in atmospheric pressure. The temperature drops two degrees. Everyone's shoulders come down an inch. The conversation gets a little more honest. You feel, without being able to explain why, that you can stop performing. That whoever you are — messy, confused, uncertain, contradictory — is acceptable in this space. That you don't have to be polished or right or finished. You can just *be*.

What is that? What is that quality? We call it "presence" sometimes, or "groundedness," or "warmth," but those words are too small. What we're actually sensing is a nervous system. A nervous system that has been through the fire enough times to know it won't die. A nervous system that has stayed — with conflict, with uncertainty, with grief, with its own messy, contradictory feelings — so many times that staying became its default instead of fleeing. That nervous system changes the room because it changes *you*. You feel its steadiness and your own nervous system downregulates in response.

That's the softened edge. And it's the most visible, most tangible, most recognizable expression of the discomfort dividend.

It is built. Not born.

When a person stops fighting reality — stops suppressing feelings, stops avoiding uncertainty, stops demanding that the world conform to their preferences, stops using certainty as a shield and comfort as a goal — something measurable happens in the nervous system. Remember the FADE pattern from Chapter 4? The shift from amygdala-driven reactivity to prefrontal-cortex-driven regulation? In the person who has trained their distress tolerance, this shift produces something extraordinary.

The prefrontal cortex doesn't just *manage* the amygdala's alarm signal. It *enriches* it. It adds context. It adds nuance. It adds time. The raw "DANGER" signal from the amygdala — which in an untrained system produces immediate fight-or-flight — gets processed through a prefrontal system that has learned to ask, "Is this actually dangerous, or is it just uncomfortable? What's the broader context? What are my options? What would the wisest version of me do right now?"

That processing takes time. Fractions of a second, but fractions of a second that change *everything*. And in those fractions — in that tiny, trainable gap between signal and response — the person's emotional experience becomes *complex* instead of simple. They don't feel one thing. They feel *several* things simultaneously. And they can hold them.

This is what people sense when they're in the presence of someone with a softened edge. They're not sensing *absence* — absence of stress, absence of emotion, absence of reaction. They're sensing *capacity*. The capacity to hold more. To feel more. To process more. To sit with contradiction without needing to resolve it. Their nervous system recognizes a nervous system that isn't fighting, and it responds by lowering its own defenses. The calm is contagious because it's genuine, and genuine calm is one of the rarest things in the world.

Here's what the softened edge is *not*: it's not flatness. It's not emotional detachment. It's not the thousand-yard stare of someone who's checked out. Some people who present as "calm" are actually suppressed — they've turned the volume so far down on their emotional life that nothing gets through. These people don't make you feel safe. They make you feel *uneasy*. Because your nervous system can detect the difference between a person who has processed their fire and a person who has simply disconnected from it. One is warm. The other is cold. And the difference matters.

The Complexity of Wisdom

This is called affective complexity, and it's one of the most underappreciated hallmarks of psychological wisdom.

Gisela Labouvie-Vief, a developmental psychologist who spent decades studying emotion and cognition across the lifespan, documented something that contradicts nearly everything popular culture tells us about wise people: **wise people don't feel fewer emotions. They feel more.** More emotions. More simultaneously. More contradictory emotions held in tension without collapsing into simplification.

Sadness and gratitude. Anger and compassion. Fear and curiosity. Regret and acceptance. The wise person doesn't resolve these contradictions. They *hold* them. They let them coexist. They sit with the discomfort of feeling two opposing things at the same time and they don't pick a side, because picking a side would mean discarding half of reality to make the other half more comfortable.

This is why wisdom doesn't look like serenity. It looks like *depth*. The serene person has simplified their emotional life — they've turned down the volume on the difficult stations so only the easy-listening channels come through. The wise person has turned up *all* the stations and learned to listen to the whole orchestra, including the discordant notes.

If your emotional life has gotten simpler as you've aged — if you feel *fewer* things, less intensely, with less contradiction — that might not be maturity. It might be suppression. And suppression, as we established in Chapter 4, is the FADE pattern gone wrong.

The Uncomfortable Truth: Wisdom doesn't feel like serenity. It feels like *complexity*. It feels like holding two contradictory truths at the same time and not collapsing into either one. If your emotional life has gotten simpler as you've aged, that might not be maturity. It might be suppression. The wise person feels MORE, not less. They just don't drown in it.

Research Spotlight: Cognitive Reappraisal

The skill that makes affective complexity possible has a name: cognitive reappraisal. Researchers Kevin Ochsner and James Gross defined it as the ability to change the *interpretation* of an emotionally charged situation without changing the situation itself.

Here's the critical distinction: reappraisal is not suppression. Suppression says, "I won't feel this." It shuts down the emotional response. Reappraisal says, "I feel this, AND I can see it from a different angle." It keeps the emotion alive while adding perspective.

Studies on reappraisal in older adults show that those who default to reappraisal (vs. suppression) maintain greater cognitive flexibility, better emotional well-being, stronger social connections, and — here's the kicker — more complex emotional experiences. They feel more. And they handle it better. Not because they're tougher. Because they've developed a prefrontal cortex that processes emotional signals with nuance instead of shutting them down.

Reappraisal is trainable. It improves with practice. And it is, in many ways, the cognitive mechanism through which the softened edge is built — one reinterpretation at a time.

The Mirror Moment

Think about the last time you felt something *complicated*. Not a clean emotion — not pure joy, pure sadness, pure anger. A *mixed* emotion. Something like sadness and relief at the same time. Or love and irritation. Or gratitude and grief.

How long did you sit with the mixture before your brain tried to simplify it? Before you picked a side? "I'm happy." "I'm upset." "I'm fine." How long before the complexity collapsed into a single, manageable label?

The length of time you can hold the mixture *without simplifying it* is a direct measure of your affective complexity. And your affective complexity is a direct measure of your wisdom.

Exercise: The Reappraisal Practice

Purpose: To practice cognitive reappraisal — changing your interpretation of a situation while staying present with the emotions it generates.

Instructions: 1. Think of a recent situation that upset you — an argument, a news story, a disappointment, a frustrating interaction. Something where you had a strong, clear emotional response. 2. Write down your initial interpretation: "What happened was [X] and it means [Y]." Be specific and honest. Don't soften it. 3. Now generate three alternative interpretations. Not "positive spin." Not "everything happens for a reason." Genuinely different ways of understanding the same event: - "What if this means [Z] instead?" - "What if I'm missing [this piece of context]?" - "What would someone I consider wise think about this?" 4. Notice: Do any of the alternative interpretations feel *true* — or at least *possible*? How does holding multiple interpretations simultaneously feel in your body compared to holding just one? 5. Now try to hold your original interpretation AND one of the alternatives at the same time. Not choosing between them. Holding both. Feel the cognitive discomfort of contradiction.

What You Might Notice: Your brain *hates* this. It wants ONE story. One interpretation. One clear assignment of blame or meaning. The discomfort of holding several simultaneously is the cognitive equivalent of holding a plank — it's shaky, it's unpleasant, and it's building exactly the neural architecture you need. If it feels like your brain is trying to flip a coin and you keep catching it mid-air and refusing to look — that's the exercise working.

Debrief: The goal isn't to replace your interpretation with a "better" one. It's to expand your capacity to hold *multiple* interpretations at once. That expansion — that tolerance for contradictory truths existing simultaneously — is the definition of affective complexity. And affective complexity is what the softened edge is made of.

Chapter Takeaway: The softened edge is what happens to a nervous system that has stopped fighting reality. The brain shifts from avoidance to regulation. Emotions become complex instead of simple. Certainty gives way to flexibility. And the person becomes, visibly and palpably, easier to be around — not because they feel less, but because they've learned to hold more.

That person in the room — the one who makes everything calmer just by being there? They weren't born that way. They were built that way. By every conversation they stayed in. Every grief they processed. Every certainty they questioned. Every time they chose to feel the hard thing instead of running from it. That's not a gift. That's a dividend.

Chapter 11

Building the Muscle

A non-clinical toolkit for people who aren't in crisis — they just don't want to become insufferable.

Look. I'm not a therapist. I have a couple of master's degrees and strong opinions, which in some professional circles makes me *more* dangerous than a therapist, not less. I'm an instructional designer by trade, which means my job is to take complicated things and make them learnable, and right now the complicated thing is "how to not become a rigid, fragile caricature of yourself by the time you're seventy."

I'm not going to pretend this chapter replaces professional help. If you need therapy, go get therapy. Seriously. Every human being should see a therapist at least once, the same way every human being should get their teeth cleaned at least once, even if nothing hurts. Especially if nothing hurts. The things that don't seem to hurt are often the things doing the most damage.

But most of the people reading this book are not in crisis. They're not diagnosable. They're just... *noticing*. Noticing that their world is getting smaller. Their patience is getting thinner. Their reactions are getting faster and less considered. Their list of things they refuse to discuss is getting longer. Their list of new experiences is getting shorter. They're not sick. They're *calcifying*. And you don't need a prescription for calcification. You need a practice.

So here's the toolkit. Six practices. All non-clinical. All evidence-informed. All designed by an instructional designer who thinks most self-help exercises are too vague to be useful and too serious to be tolerable. Let me walk you through each one with enough specificity that you can actually do them, because "be more open" is not a practice. It's a bumper sticker.

A note on the design: these practices are scaffolded. That means they're organized from lowest-threshold (the Pause Protocol, which you can do without anyone knowing you're doing it) to highest-threshold (the Novelty Requirement, which asks you to do something new every week for the rest of your life). You don't have to do all six. You don't even have to do three. Pick two. The two that make you most uncomfortable — because the discomfort is, as we have now established beyond any reasonable doubt, the point. Do them for thirty days. Not forever. Thirty days. Then evaluate. Adjust. Continue. This is instructional design, not religion. We iterate. We don't canonize.

One more thing: none of these practices will work if you do them perfectly and none of them will fail if you do them imperfectly. The practice is the point. The showing up is the point. If you do the Pause Protocol three times in a week when you committed to five, you didn't fail — you paused three more times than you would have without the commitment. Three reps is three more than zero. We're not grading here. We're growing.

Practice 1: The Pause Protocol

What it is: A deliberate ten-second gap between stimulus and response in any triggering moment.

How to do it: 1. When triggered — irritated, defensive, angry, anxious, certain — notice the trigger. This is harder than it sounds because the trigger often fires below conscious awareness. The physical signs are your early warning system: jaw tightens, shoulders rise, chest gets hot, breathing shallows. 2. Say internally: *"Pause."* 3. Take one slow breath. In through the nose, out through the mouth. This is not meditation. This is buying time. 4. Ask yourself three questions, in order: *"What *am I feeling right now?"* (Name the emotion, even roughly.) *"What do I want to do?"* (Name the impulse — leave, argue, fix, deflect, attack.) *"Is there another option?"* 5. Choose. You might still do the impulsive thing. That's fine. The pause is the point, not the outcome.

When: Daily. Every triggering moment is an opportunity. Start with one deliberate pause per day. Build to three. Don't try for ten — that's how practices die.

Practice 2: The "What Would I Need to See?" Exercise

What it is: For any strong opinion, establishing a personal falsifiability standard.

How to do it: 1. Pick one opinion you hold strongly. The stronger the better. The one that makes your voice change when someone challenges it. 2. Write this sentence and complete it: *"I would change my mind about this if I saw _____."* 3. If the blank stays empty — if there is truly *nothing* that could change your mind — you've identified a locked door. That's not a strong belief. That's a defended position. 4. For locked doors, ask the follow-up: *What would it cost me to be wrong about this?* What identity, relationship, or worldview is this opinion protecting? The cost reveals the function. The function reveals the avoidance.

When: Weekly. One opinion per week. Keep a running list. Over time, the list becomes a map of your rigidity — and your growth.

Practice 3: The Discomfort Journal

What it is: A daily log of moments you avoided discomfort — not to shame yourself, but to notice patterns.

How to do it: 1. Every evening, spend two minutes writing down one to three moments from the day where you noticed emotional discomfort. 2. For each, note four things: (a) The trigger, (b) The feeling, (c) What you did — stayed or fled, (d) What the avoidance cost you, if anything. 3. No judgment. No grades. No improvement goals. This is *data collection*, not self-improvement. You're mapping the terrain before you start hiking.

When: Daily for fourteen days. Then stop and review the log. Look for patterns. Which arena (kitchen table, news feed, body, silence) shows the most avoidance? Which emotions trigger the fastest escapes? Which escape strategies are most automatic? The patterns will tell you where your practice needs to focus.

Practice 4: The Perspective Swap

What it is: Deliberately engaging with a viewpoint that feels wrong to you — reading, watching, or listening to the *best* version of an argument you disagree with.

How to do it: 1. Once a week, consume one piece of high-quality content that represents a viewpoint you strongly disagree with. Not the straw man. The *steel man*. The most thoughtful, most credible version of the opposing argument you can find. 2. Read or listen to the entire thing without interrupting internally. No rebuttals mid-sentence. No eye-rolls. No hate-reading. Engage with it the way you'd engage with something from your own side — looking for what's valid, what's interesting, what you hadn't considered. 3. After consuming it, write three things: (a) One point that was stronger than expected. (b) One thing you still disagree with — but can articulate *why*. (c) One thing you learned about why *you* hold your position.

When: Weekly. One swap per week. The goal isn't to change your mind. The goal is to prove to yourself that engaging with the other side is *survivable* — and that surviving it makes your own position either stronger (because it was tested) or different (because you learned something).

Practice 5: The Micro-Suck

What it is: Choosing one small thing you don't want to do each day — not for the outcome, but for the aMCC activation.

How to do it: 1. Every morning, identify one thing on your list — or not on your list — that you genuinely don't want to do. It should be small, manageable, and non-harmful. We're not talking about running a marathon or confronting your deepest trauma. We're talking about the email you've been avoiding. The phone call you keep postponing. The drawer you refuse to clean. The walk in weather you don't prefer. 2. Do it *first*. Before the reward. Before the comfortable task. Before the thing you actually want to do. 3. Notice the resistance as you do it. That resistance — that internal "I don't wanna" — is the aMCC activating. That's the rep. The outcome of the task is irrelevant. The resistance is the workout.

When: Daily. One micro-suck per day. Every day. Non-negotiable. This is the push-up of the discomfort dividend program.

Practice 6: The Novelty Requirement

What it is: Building one genuinely new experience per week into your life. Not expensive. Not dramatic. Not Instagram-worthy. Just *unfamiliar*.

How to do it: 1. Once a week, do something you've never done before. The bar is low on purpose. Cook a cuisine you've never attempted. Take a different route to work. Go to a store you've never entered. Start a conversation with a stranger. Read a book in a genre you'd normally dismiss. Watch a show in a language you don't speak. Listen to music from a tradition you don't understand. Go to a worship service for a faith you don't practice. 2. The point isn't the activity. The point is the *unfamiliarity*. Your aMCC grows when you encounter novelty. Routine — even good, comfortable, well-optimized routine — is the aMCC's natural enemy. Novelty is its food.

When: Weekly. One new thing per week. Put it on the calendar like an appointment. Because it is one — an appointment with your own growth.

Exercise: Design Your Practice Plan

Purpose: To select two or three practices from the toolkit and commit to a specific, time-bound protocol.

Instructions:

1. Review the six practices above.
2. Select two or three that target your primary arena of need. If your biggest challenge is family conflict, start with the Pause Protocol and the Discomfort Journal. If it's intellectual rigidity, start with the Perspective Swap and the "What Would I Need to See?" exercise. If it's social isolation, start with the Novelty Requirement and the Conversation Bridge from Chapter 8. If it's everything — start with the Micro-Suck (because it covers all arenas) and the Discomfort Journal (because it gives you data).
3. Write a commitment statement: *"For the next 30 days, I will practice [Practice A] [frequency] and [Practice B] [frequency]."*
4. Put it somewhere visible. Set a calendar reminder for day 30.
5. At thirty days, evaluate: What changed? What was harder than expected? What was easier? What's next?

Debrief: Thirty days isn't arbitrary. It's long enough to build a groove, short enough to be psychologically survivable, and specific enough to generate real data about what works for you. At thirty days, you're not done — you're *calibrated*. You know which practices land and which don't. You know where your resistance is strongest and where it's starting to soften. That information is the foundation for everything that comes next.

Chapter Takeaway: You don't need a crisis or a diagnosis to build distress tolerance. You need a practice. Pick two. Do them for thirty days. The practices are small. The compound interest is enormous. And the barrier to entry is zero — just the willingness to be slightly uncomfortable, slightly more often, for slightly longer than you'd prefer.

I'm not asking you to go to therapy. I mean, you probably should — everybody should — but that's not the assignment. The assignment is smaller. Tomorrow morning, before you reach for your phone, sit with whatever you're feeling for sixty seconds. It might be nothing. It might be everything. Either way, just stay.

PART IV: THE DIVIDEND

What you get for all this staying

Chapter 12

The Discomfort Dividend

What you actually get for all this staying.

So what do you actually *get* for all this?

I've spent eleven chapters telling you that the world's most important skill involves voluntarily sitting in rooms that make you uncomfortable, questioning beliefs that make you feel safe, reading things that make your blood pressure spike, tolerating silence that makes you squirm, and having conversations that make you want to fake a heart attack just to have an excuse to leave. I've told you your brain has a muscle that only grows when you do things you hate. I've told you certainty is cocaine. I've told you your intelligence is building walls instead of bridges. I've told you grief is the admission price and the silence test is the bar exam and your aMCC is shrinking while you watch Netflix.

That's a *lot* of bad news across a lot of pages. You deserve some good news.

Here it is: the dividend is real. It's measurable. It's multi-dimensional. And once it starts paying out, it pays out in every area of your life simultaneously, like an investment that earns compound interest in four currencies at once.

Currency One: Better Decisions

People with high distress tolerance and ambiguity tolerance make better decisions. Not because they're smarter — we buried that myth in Chapter 2. Not because they're more logical

— logic is a tool, and tools work for whoever picks them up. They make better decisions because they can *wait*.

They can sit in the uncertainty of a complex problem long enough for better information to emerge. They don't rush to closure. They don't grab the first answer that reduces their anxiety. They don't seize and freeze — locking in a judgment before all the evidence is in because the discomfort of not-knowing was too much to bear.

They wait. And the waiting — which is itself a distress tolerance skill, which is itself an aMCC workout, which is itself an act of remarkable psychological courage — produces better outcomes. Not always. Not magically. But consistently. The person who can tolerate the discomfort of an open question for an extra hour, an extra day, an extra week, is the person who makes the decision with more data, more perspective, and less desperation.

Every great decision you've ever seen someone make — in business, in relationships, in life — was made by someone who could sit with "I don't know" longer than the people around them. That's not intelligence. That's endurance in the face of ambiguity. That's the dividend.

Currency Two: Richer Relationships

People who can tolerate disagreement, complexity, and emotional messiness maintain deeper, more honest, more durable relationships. They can have the hard conversation — the one where nobody's clearly right and somebody's feelings are going to get bruised — without needing to win it, avoid it, or fix it. They can hold space for someone else's pain without immediately trying to make it stop. They can love people who are different from them without requiring those people to change.

Their relationships are bridges, not echo chambers. They have friends who disagree with them. They have family members they don't understand but haven't given up on. They have the kind of marriages where both people can say "I don't know how to fix this and I'm not going anywhere" and mean both halves of the sentence.

This is not natural. This is not default human behavior. This is *trained*. Every stayed conversation, every tolerated disagreement, every moment of listening without fixing — it compounds. And the person who has compounded enough of these moments doesn't just have better relationships. They have *different* relationships. Deeper ones. Messier ones. More honest ones. The kind where both people can be wrong and nobody has to leave.

Currency Three: Reduced Death Anxiety

This one surprises people. But the data is consistent, and the logic is airtight.

Death anxiety is, at its core, an ambiguity intolerance problem. The fear of death is, in most people, not primarily a fear of pain or suffering. It's a fear of *not knowing*. Not knowing what comes next. Not knowing if there's anything at all. Not knowing if your life mattered. Not knowing if you'll be remembered. The ultimate open question, with no possibility of resolution before the exam.

If you've spent decades *avoiding* ambiguity — building walls of certainty, filtering out uncomfortable questions, refusing to sit with "I don't know" — death is the question you can't escape. It's the open loop that no amount of closure can close. And the anxiety it produces is proportional to how badly you need closure to feel safe.

But if you've spent decades *practicing* ambiguity tolerance — carrying open questions, sitting with uncertainty, learning that not-knowing is survivable — death becomes something different. Not comfortable. Not welcome. But *tolerable*. You've practiced sitting with the ultimate "I don't know" without collapsing. You've proven, thousands of times, that uncertainty is survivable. And the biggest uncertainty of all — the one that awaits everyone — becomes less terrifying. Not because you've solved it. Because you've practiced not needing to solve things in order to live with them.

I've watched this play out in real life. The people I know who are most at peace with mortality are not the ones with the strongest religious convictions or the most elaborate philosophical frameworks. They're the ones who have spent their lives developing the capacity to sit with questions that don't have answers. They didn't make death *certain* — they didn't resolve it into heaven or oblivion or reincarnation or any other comforting narrative. They made *uncertainty itself* less frightening. And since death is the ultimate uncertainty, the fear lost its stranglehold.

That's not enlightenment. That's compound interest on decades of ten-second stays.

Currency Four: Grace

This is the hardest to measure and the easiest to see. It's what I described in the opening of Chapter 10 — that quality that certain people carry, the one that changes the room. The softened edge made visible.

Wise people move through the world differently. There's a quality to it — a slowness, a steadiness, a groundedness that isn't performed or practiced but *is*. They're not pretending to be calm. They are calm — not because nothing bothers them, but because they've been bothered enough times to know that being bothered is survivable.

Grace shows up in posture. In tone. In pace. In the way a person holds eye contact without aggression. In the way they ask questions with genuine curiosity instead of rhetorical purpose. In the way they respond to provocation with patience instead of counter-attack. In the way they hold space for complexity instead of collapsing it into simplicity.

You can't fake it. You can only earn it. And you earn it through thousands of reps of staying when everything in you wanted to leave. That's the dividend. Visible, palpable, room-changing.

The Mirror Moment

Rate yourself, honestly, on each dividend domain. One to five. One means "not at all," five means "consistently."

- **Decisions:** "I can sit with uncertainty long enough to make thoughtful decisions instead of reactive ones."
- **Relationships:** "I can be in a relationship with someone who disagrees with me without needing to change them or leave."
- **Mortality:** "I can think about my own death without significant anxiety or avoidance."
- **Grace:** "People around me feel calmer, not more activated, after spending time with me."

Notice which domain is your highest and which is your lowest. The lowest is your next practice target. The highest is evidence that the dividend is already paying out.

The Uncomfortable Truth: The dividend isn't enlightenment. It's not floating above the chaos. It's walking into a room full of people who disagree with you and feeling your pulse stay at 72. It's hearing news that scares you and being able to *think* instead of react. It's looking at the end of your life and feeling something other than panic. That's not flashy. But it's everything.

One more distinction before we close this chapter, because it matters.

There's a difference between a bridge that *bends* and a bridge that *holds rigid until it breaks.*

The rigid bridge looks strong. It looks solid. It looks like it can handle anything. And it can — up to a point. But when the load exceeds its capacity, it doesn't flex. It *shatters.* Catastrophically. Without warning. The thing that looked like strength was actually brittleness.

The flexible bridge looks less impressive. It sways in the wind. It moves under load. It bends when pressure is applied. It doesn't *look* strong. But it absorbs force instead of resisting it. It distributes load instead of concentrating it. And when the storm comes — the storm that breaks the rigid bridge — the flexible bridge is still standing. Swaying, maybe. Creaking, probably. But standing.

Endurance is the rigid bridge. "I can take it. I can survive anything. I don't bend." Endurance looks like strength from the outside and produces shattering from the inside.

Resilience is the flexible bridge. "I can bend. I can absorb. I can let the force move through me instead of building up inside me." Resilience doesn't look as impressive, but it survives what endurance cannot.

The discomfort dividend doesn't produce endurance. It produces resilience. The ability to bend without breaking. To feel without shattering. To sit with the storm without becoming rigid against it.

That's the payoff. Not that you can survive anything. That you can *bend* through anything. And keep standing.

Chapter Takeaway: The discomfort dividend pays out in four currencies: better decisions (because you can wait), richer relationships (because you can stay), reduced death anxiety (because you've practiced not-knowing), and grace (because your nervous system has been trained by fire). You don't earn it by reading about it. You earn it one rep at a time.

The dividend isn't flashy. There's no trophy. No ceremony. No moment where the clouds part and you float. It's quieter than that. It's the moment you realize you're not scared anymore. Not of being wrong. Not of being uncertain. Not even of being gone. That's the dividend. And it's worth every uncomfortable second that bought it.

Chapter 13

The Final Unfolding

Why the work never ends — and why that's the whole point.

I have some bad news and some good news.

The bad news: there's no finish line.

You don't get to a point where you're "wise enough" and can stop doing the work. You don't graduate from the discomfort program and receive a certificate and spend the rest of your days floating serenely above the fray, dispensing wisdom like a human fortune cookie. There is no level of distress tolerance where the discomfort stops being uncomfortable. There is no amount of ambiguity tolerance where not-knowing stops feeling like free-fall. There is no aMCC thickness at which the hard thing becomes easy permanently.

The moment you feel finished — the moment you sit back and think *I've arrived, I've figured it out, I'm done* — is the moment the concentration process starts again. Comfort creeps in. The aMCC starts thinning. The certainty starts flowing. The walls start going back up. The broth starts concentrating around the same old ingredients. Because the default direction of aging hasn't changed just because you read a book. The gravity is still pulling toward closure, toward comfort, toward the shrinking room. You've learned to resist the gravity. But the gravity doesn't stop.

That's the bad news.

Here's the good news: that's the whole point.

The Garden That Never Stops Growing

If wisdom had a finish line, it wouldn't be wisdom. It would be a degree. You'd earn it, frame it, hang it on the wall, and stop learning. You'd "know enough" and settle into the knowing like a warm bath. And the warm bath would slowly, imperceptibly, become a cage — because that's what all closed systems become eventually.

The fact that wisdom never ends — that there is always a harder conversation to have, a deeper uncertainty to tolerate, a more challenging belief to question, a more painful grief to process — is not a burden. It's the architecture of a life that keeps expanding instead of contracting.

Wisdom is a garden, not a trophy case. You don't display it. You tend it. Every day. In weather you don't prefer. With dirt under your nails. And the garden doesn't stop growing just because you took a weekend off. If you stop tending it, it doesn't stay the same — it goes wild, or it dies. There is no maintenance-free wisdom. There is no set-it-and-forget-it enlightenment.

And that — I promise you — is not depressing. That is liberating. Because it means the work is always available. The gym is always open. The fire is always burning. No matter how far you've come, there's always another rep. Another stayed conversation. Another tolerated ambiguity. Another moment of choosing presence over escape.

You never run out of material. Life guarantees it.

The Calibration Principle

Judith Glück's research on the MORE model contains a finding that most people miss entirely, and it might be the most important finding in this entire book.

For all five wisdom resources — managing uncertainty, openness, reflectivity, emotional sensitivity, and emotion regulation — **the optimal level is not the maximum.**

Read that again. Let it land.

You can be so aware of uncertainty that you become paralyzed. Unable to make decisions. Unable to commit to anything because you can always see one more complication, one more angle, one more reason to wait. Ambiguity tolerance taken to its extreme becomes indecision.

You can be so open to others' views that you can't hold your own. So willing to consider every perspective that you lose your center. So receptive to new information that you blow with every wind. Openness taken to its extreme becomes spinelessness.

You can be so reflective that you lose all confidence. So busy examining your own motives and assumptions that you can't act. So self-critical that you question yourself into inaction. Reflectivity taken to its extreme becomes rumination.

You can be so sensitive to emotions — your own and others' — that you burn out. So attuned to every feeling in the room that you absorb all of it and have nothing left. Emotional sensitivity taken to its extreme becomes overwhelm.

Wisdom is not about maximizing any single capacity. It's about *calibrating* — finding the dynamic, shifting balance between openness and groundedness. Between feeling and regulation. Between knowing and not-knowing. Between staying and leaving. Between holding on and letting go.

That calibration is never static. It changes with every new experience. Every new loss. Every new relationship. Every new decade. The wisdom of fifty is not the wisdom of seventy. The flexibility you need in a crisis is not the flexibility you need in contentment. The openness that serves you in a new job is not the openness that serves you in a long marriage.

The work of wisdom is the work of ongoing adjustment — perpetually recalibrating your relationship with discomfort, uncertainty, and complexity based on what life is handing you *right now*. Not what it handed you last year. Not what you expect it to hand you next year. *Right now*.

The person who thinks they've figured it out is the person who's stopped calibrating. And the person who's stopped calibrating is the person who's started concentrating again.

The Uncomfortable Truth: If you've read this entire book and feel comfortable — I failed. If you've read this entire book and feel slightly unsettled, slightly less certain, slightly more aware of the ways you've been avoiding the fire — welcome. That unsettled feeling isn't a problem. That's the dividend starting to accrue.

Research Spotlight: The Seeds and the Harvest

The longitudinal data on wisdom development tells a story that is both humbling and hopeful. Wink and Helson (1997) followed individuals from young adulthood into later life and found that psychological mindedness and openness measured in the twenties and thirties positively predicted wisdom decades later. The seeds, it seems, are planted early.

But seeds need tending. And the Glück research shows that the tending never stops. The most wisdom-scoring participants in her studies weren't the ones who had the most openness or the most reflectivity or the most emotional regulation. They were the ones who had the right *balance* — and who kept adjusting that balance as their lives changed. They were perpetual gardeners. Not finished products.

The implication is clear: wherever you are right now — whatever seeds you planted or failed to plant in your twenties and thirties — the garden can still grow. It might need more work. The soil might need more amending. But the capacity for growth doesn't expire. It just requires that you never stop showing up with the shovel.

The Mirror Moment

One last question. The hardest one. The one this whole book has been building toward.

Are you still unfolding, or have you started folding up?

Not who you were five years ago. Not who you plan to be next year. Right now. Today. This week. Are you expanding or contracting? Opening or closing? Moving toward discomfort or away from it?

Don't answer with what you want the answer to be. Answer with what's true.

And then decide what you want to do about it.

Exercise: The Letter to Your Future Self

Purpose: To create a personal commitment artifact — a time capsule of intention that you'll encounter again in one year, holding you accountable to the person you're choosing to become.

Instructions:

1. Write a letter to yourself, dated one year from today. This is not a goal-setting exercise. It's an *honesty* exercise. In the letter, address the following:

    -   **What were you like when you started this book?** Not the flattering version. The honest one. Where were you rigid? Where were you avoiding? What were you using as a certainty narcotic? What conversations were you fleeing?

- **What surprised you?** What idea, finding, or exercise in this book landed in a place you didn't expect? What did you learn about yourself that you weren't planning to learn?

- **What practice are you committing to?** Not all six. Not even three. Which one or two from the toolkit are you taking with you? Write them down. Be specific about frequency.

- **What are you most afraid of avoiding?** Name the conversation, the question, the loss, the uncertainty that you know is waiting for you and that you're most tempted to flee from. Name it.

- **What do you hope is different one year from now?** Not in your circumstances — you can't control those. In your *capacity*. Your ability to stay. Your willingness to not-know. Your tolerance for the fire.

2. Seal the letter. Write the open date on the outside. If you want to be extra accountable, put a calendar reminder in your phone.

3. Put it somewhere you'll find it in a year. A drawer you open regularly. A book you'll reread. A trusted friend's hands with instructions to return it on the date.

4. When you open it in a year: Were you right about what would be hard? What changed? What didn't? Are you still doing the work? Did the discomfort dividend start paying out?

What You Might Notice: This exercise asks you to tolerate a very specific kind of ambiguity — the most personal kind. You don't know who you'll be in a year. You can't control how the letter will feel when you open it. You can't guarantee that you'll have done the work. You have to trust the process — and the person you're choosing to become — without seeing the destination. That trust, in and of itself, is a final act of distress tolerance. You're sitting with the ultimate open question: *Who am I becoming?*

Debrief: The letter isn't the point. The *writing* is the point. The act of articulating what you want to change — and committing to it in writing, with a future-dated accountability check — moves the intention from "I should probably do something" to "I'm doing something." Words on paper have weight. They have mass. They resist the gravity of forgetting in a way that thoughts do not. Use them

---

What This Book Was Really About

Let me tell you what this book was really about. Not the science — though the science matters. Not the exercises — though the exercises work. Not the research or the frameworks or the brain structures or the clinical terminology.

This book was about one thing: staying.

Staying in the conversation when you want to leave. Staying with the question when you want an answer. Staying with the feeling when you want it to stop. Staying with the uncertainty when you want the certainty like you want oxygen. Staying with the loss when you want to move on. Staying with yourself when the silence gets loud and the mirror gets honest and the version of you that stares back isn't the version you were hoping to see.

Every chapter was a variation on the same theme. Every exercise was a different angle on the same skill. Every piece of research pointed to the same conclusion: the people who age into wisdom are the people who stay. Not the smartest. Not the most educated. Not the most successful. The ones who stay.

And staying never gets easy. It gets *easier*. The tenth second becomes less agonizing than the first. The hundredth rep is smoother than the tenth. The aMCC grows. The tolerance builds. The edge softens. But the discomfort doesn't disappear. Because life doesn't stop generating discomfort. It can't. That's what life *is* — a continuous, inexhaustible supply of moments that demand something from you that you'd rather not give.

The people who give it anyway — who stay in the fire, who carry the question, who hold the contradiction, who feel the grief, who tolerate the silence, who say "I don't know" without collapsing — those people earn the dividend. Not once. In perpetuity. Because the work never stops, and neither does the return.

Chapter Takeaway: Wisdom is not a destination. It's a practice. The work never ends because life never stops being ambiguous, uncomfortable, and uncertain. The person who embraces that — who sees the perpetual unfolding not as a burden but as the *structure* of a meaningful life — is the person who earns the discomfort dividend in perpetuity. Everyone else is just waiting for the concrete to set.

You are never done unfolding. The day you decide you're done is the day you start folding up. Stay uncomfortable. Stay curious. Stay in the room. The fire doesn't kill you. The leaving does.

End of The Discomfort Dividend

Every major claim in this book is grounded in peer-reviewed research. Below is a plain-language summary of each key study cited, organized by research pillar, followed by a complete bibliography. For each study: who did it, what they found, and why a non-scientist should care.

Pillar A: The Neuroscience

1. The Anterior Midcingulate Cortex (aMCC) — "The Stubbornness Muscle" The aMCC is a network hub that performs cost/benefit computations necessary for tenacity — persistence in the face of challenge. It integrates signals from systems involved in attention, reward, memory, emotion, and motor control. Superagers (older adults who perform cognitively at the level of people decades younger) tend to have larger, more connected aMCCs. The aMCC grows when you do things you don't want to do and shrinks when you stop challenging yourself. Once a challenging activity becomes enjoyable, aMCC activation diminishes — growth requires ongoing novelty of discomfort.

Primary Source: Touroutoglou, A., Andreano, J., Dickerson, B. C., & Barrett, L. F. (2020). "The tenacious brain: How the anterior mid-cingulate contributes to achieving goals." Cortex, 123, 12–29.

Used in: Chapters 3, 5, 9, 11, 12

2. The FADE Hypothesis — "The Fork in the Brain" FADE stands for Fronto-Amygdalar Age-Related Differences in Emotion. As the brain ages, the amygdala becomes less active in response to negative stimuli while the prefrontal cortex becomes more active. This shift can reflect genuine emotional regulation (adaptive) or emotional suppression/avoidance (maladaptive). The variable that determines which trajectory you follow is distress tolerance.

Primary Source: St. Jacques, P. L., Bessette-Symons, B., & Cabeza, R. (2009). "Functional neuroimaging studies of aging and emotion: Fronto-amygdalar differences during emotional perception and episodic memory." Journal of the International Neuropsychological Society, 15(6), 819–825.

Used in: Chapters 4, 10

Pillar B: The Psychology

3. The MORE Life Experience Model — "The Wisdom Recipe" Why do some people become wiser through life's challenges while most do not? Glück and Bluck identified five psychological resources that determine whether adversity leads to growth or entrenchment: Managing uncertainty (M), Openness (O), Reflectivity (R), and Emotional Sensitivity/Emotion Regulation/Empathy (E). Critical finding: for all five resources, the optimal level is not the maximum. Wisdom is calibration, not extremity.

Primary Sources: Glück, J., & Bluck, S. (2013). "The MORE Life Experience Model." In Ferrari & Weststrate (Eds.), The Scientific Study of Personal Wisdom. Springer. | Glück, J. (2018). "More on the MORE Life Experience Model: What We Have Learned (So Far)." The Journal of Value Inquiry, 53, 349–370.

Used in: Chapters 6, 7, 10, 13

4. The 2025 Ambiguity–Wisdom Study Ambiguity tolerance positively predicts psychological well-being through a sequential mediation chain: ambiguity tolerance → epistemic curiosity → wisdom → well-being. Your ability to sit with "I don't know" makes you curious, curiosity builds wisdom, and wisdom predicts well-being. The chain only works if the first link holds.

Primary Source: Shi, J., Liu, Y., Xu, W., & Tang, Y. (2025). "The influence of ambiguity tolerance on psychological well-being: The roles of interest-type epistemic curiosity and wisdom." Personality and Individual Differences / Acta Psychologica, 242.

Used in: Chapters 2, 6

5. Distress Tolerance and Psychological Flexibility A systematic review of 106 studies found that interventions (mindfulness, ACT, DBT, CBT) consistently reduced distress intolerance, and reductions predicted greater psychological flexibility. The skill is trainable at any age. Separately, Kashdan and Rottenberg established psychological flexibility as a fundamental aspect of health, showing that people who are open and curious about their emotional experiences pursue richer, more meaningful lives.

Primary Sources: Systematic review, Cognitive Therapy and Research (2023). | Kashdan, T. B., & Rottenberg, J. (2010). "Psychological flexibility as a fundamental aspect of health." Clinical Psychology Review, 30(7), 865–878. | Simons, J. S., & Gaher, R. M. (2005). The Distress Tolerance Scale. Journal of Psychopathology and Behavioral Assessment, 27(2), 83–102.

Used in: Chapters 5, 11

6. Social Rigidity in Old Age Social rigidity — the inability to adapt how you engage with other people — is significantly linked to poorer life adjustment in older adults. Crucially, it responds to intervention. The pattern can be changed.

Primary Source: Canadian Journal on Aging: "Cognitive versus social rigidity in old age: Implications for therapy." | Supporting: Seattle Longitudinal Study (Schaie & Willis).

Used in: Chapter 8

Pillar C: Aging and Emotion

7. Socioemotional Selectivity Theory and The Positivity Effect As people perceive their remaining time as limited, they prioritize emotionally meaningful goals, leading to a documented preference for positive over negative information. This book argues the positivity effect is a double-edged sword: through genuine regulation, it's adaptive; through avoidance, it becomes the engine of fragility.

Primary Sources: Carstensen, L. L., Fung, H. H., & Charles, S. T. (2003). "Socioemotional selectivity theory and the regulation of emotion in the second half of life." Motivation and Emotion, 27(2), 103–123. | Mather, M., & Carstensen, L. L. (2005). "Aging and motivated cognition: The positivity effect in attention and memory." Trends in Cognitive Sciences, 9(10), 496–502.

Used in: Chapters 1, 4, 8

8. Affective Complexity Wise people don't experience fewer emotions — they experience more, simultaneously. The capacity to hold contradictory feelings is a hallmark of psychological maturity and a direct product of distress tolerance training.

Primary Sources: Labouvie-Vief, G. (2003). "Dynamic integration: Affect, cognition, and the self in adulthood." Current Directions in Psychological Science, 12(6), 201–206. | Ong, A. D., & Bergeman, C. S. (2004). "The complexity of emotions in later life." Journals of Gerontology: Psychological Sciences, 59B(3), 117–122.

Used in: Chapters 10, 12

Pillar D: Additional Research

9. Cognitive Reappraisal. The ability to change the interpretation of an emotionally charged situation. Older adults who use reappraisal (vs. suppression) show better emotional outcomes and maintain greater cognitive flexibility. *Source: Ochsner, K. N., & Gross, J. J. (2005). Trends in Cognitive Sciences, 9(5), 242–249.*

10. Hard-Earned Wisdom. Wiser individuals process life challenges through exploratory processing (seeking meaning and growth) rather than closure processing (putting the experience behind them as quickly as possible). Adversity alone doesn't build wisdom. Adversity plus staying does. *Source: Weststrate, N. M., Ferrari, M., & Ardelt, M. (2016). Personality and Social Psychology Bulletin, 42(5), 662–676.*

11. The Berlin Wisdom Paradigm. Neither personality nor intelligence alone predicted wisdom. What did? The interface between them — creativity, cognitive style, and the willingness to engage with complexity. *Source: Baltes, P. B., & Staudinger, U. M. (2000). American Psychologist, 55(1), 122–136.*

12. Need for Cognitive Closure. People high in need for closure "seize" on early information and "freeze" on it, relying more on stereotypes and showing increased dogmatism. Need for closure increases with stress, fatigue, and time pressure — all of which become more common with age. *Source: Kruglanski, A. W., & Webster, D. M. (1996). Psychological Review, 103(2), 263–283.*

13. Personality Stability Across the Lifespan. Personality traits are remarkably stable across adulthood, but most people become slightly less open with age. The decline is a tendency, not a law — some people buck it entirely. *Source: Roberts, B. W., Walton, K. E., & Viechtbauer, W. (2006). Psychological Bulletin, 132(1), 1–25.*

14. Loneliness and Mortality. Chronic social isolation carries mortality risks equivalent to smoking 15 cigarettes a day. *Source: Holt-Lunstad, J., Smith, T. B., Baker, M., Harris, T., & Stephenson, D. (2015). Perspectives on Psychological Science, 10(2), 227–237.*

15. Wisdom and Aging Longitudinal Data. Openness and psychological mindedness in early adulthood positively predict wisdom in later life. The seeds of wisdom are planted decades before the harvest. *Source: Wink, P., & Helson, R. (1997). Journal of Adult Development. | Ardelt, M. (2003). Research on Aging, 25, 275–324. | Ardelt, M. (2011). In Schaie & Willis (Eds.), Handbook of the Psychology of Aging.*

Appendix B: Recommended Reading

Thinking, Fast and Slow by Daniel Kahneman — Read this if you want to understand why your brain lies to you for a living.

The Body Keeps the Score by Bessel van der Kolk — Read this if you suspect your body has been keeping receipts on everything your brain has been avoiding.

Atomic Habits by James Clear — Read this if you need someone to explain compounding in a way that doesn't involve a financial advisor.

The Grace in Aging by Kathleen Dowling Singh — Read this if you want the Buddhist version. Beautiful. Zero sarcasm. The opposite of this book in every way except the conclusion.

Psychological Flexibility as a Fundamental Aspect of Health by Kashdan & Rottenberg — Read this if you want the academic paper that started it all. It's free. It's dense. It's worth it.

The Scientific Study of Personal Wisdom edited by Ferrari & Weststrate — Read this if you want to know everything Glück and Bluck discovered. Academic but readable. Your book club will hate you.

Ken Konet, M.Ed., MBA is a corporate instructional designer, author, and publisher who has spent his career doing two things: designing learning experiences that actually change how adults think and behave, and writing books that refuse to talk down to their readers.

With three master's degrees — including an M.Ed. and an MBA — Ken brings a rare combination of educational design expertise, business pragmatism, and the kind of unfiltered honesty that comes from believing adults deserve to be treated like adults, even when the topic is uncomfortable. Especially when the topic is uncomfortable.

Humbolton Press is an independent publishing imprint spanning nonfiction, fiction, children's literature, and genre fiction. Ken's nonfiction work focuses on the gap between what research knows and what regular people have access to — translating clinical and academic findings into books that are rigorous, accessible, and occasionally funny enough to make you forget you're learning something.

His other nonfiction titles include:

Adults Don't Exist — A sharp, funny examination of the myth of "having it all figured out" and why the pressure to perform adulthood is making everyone worse at actually living. Part psychology, part manifesto, all Ken Mode.

The Happiness Algorithm — A research-driven guide to understanding what actually predicts well-being (spoiler: it's not what the wellness industry is selling you) and how to build a life that works for your brain instead of against it.

The Whole Child — A parenting and education book grounded in emotional intelligence research, designed for parents and educators who want to raise humans who can *feel* as well as they can *think*. Because the world has enough smart people who can't sit with a hard conversation.

Migraines Demystified — A comprehensive, patient-centered guide to understanding and managing migraines, co-developed with clinical contributor Elliott James, APRN. Written for the person who's tired of being told "it's just a headache."

Cervicogenic Migraine: The Missing Diagnosis — Ken's most personal nonfiction work, born from his own experience with chronic daily headache driven by cervical spine pathology. Part medical guide, part patient advocacy, part "why didn't anyone tell me this sooner."

Gamify Your Life for Success (with Isabella Green and Ibrahim Roble) — A practical framework for applying game design principles to personal development, goal-setting, and habit formation. Because if your brain responds to points, levels, and progress bars, you might as well use that.

Bullies Run the World (as Paul Green, M.Ed.) — A no-holds-barred examination of how bullying dynamics scale from the schoolyard to the boardroom to the political stage, and what it costs us when we normalize dominance as leadership.

Ken lives in Florida with his wife Isabella. When he's not writing, designing learning programs, or arguing with his aMCC about whether to do the hard thing, he can be found on a motorcycle, on a hiking trail, or learning to play video games significantly later in life than most people — because novelty, as this book argues, is the aMCC's favorite food.

For more information about Ken's work and Humbolton Press titles, visit [Humbolton Press website — TBD].

Humbolton Press

The Discomfort Dividend: Why the Smartest Thing You Can Do as You Age Is Stop Running from What Hurts

© 2026 Ken Konet. All rights reserved.